Cuddly Capybaras

Cute & Cozy Coloring Book

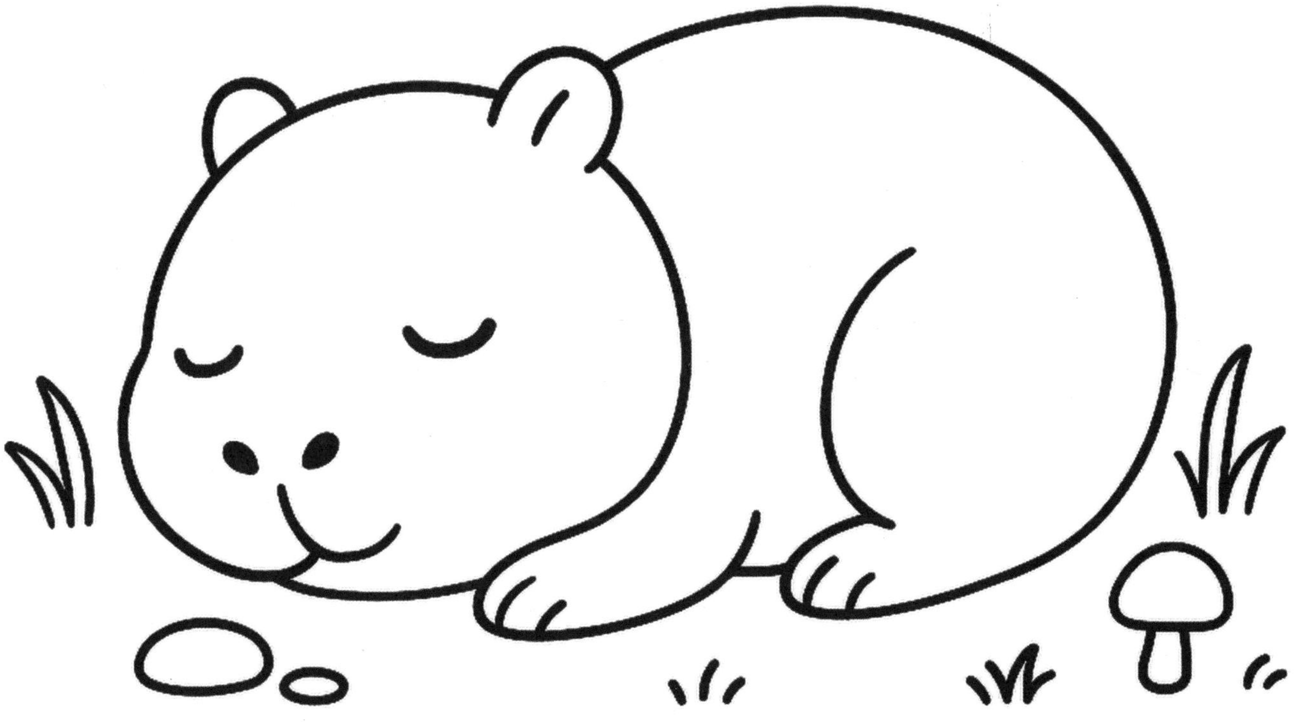

Kari Juna

Cuddly Capybaras
Distributed by Osiris Inc. / Osiris America Inc.
Printed in China
ISBN 979-8-9997005-1-3

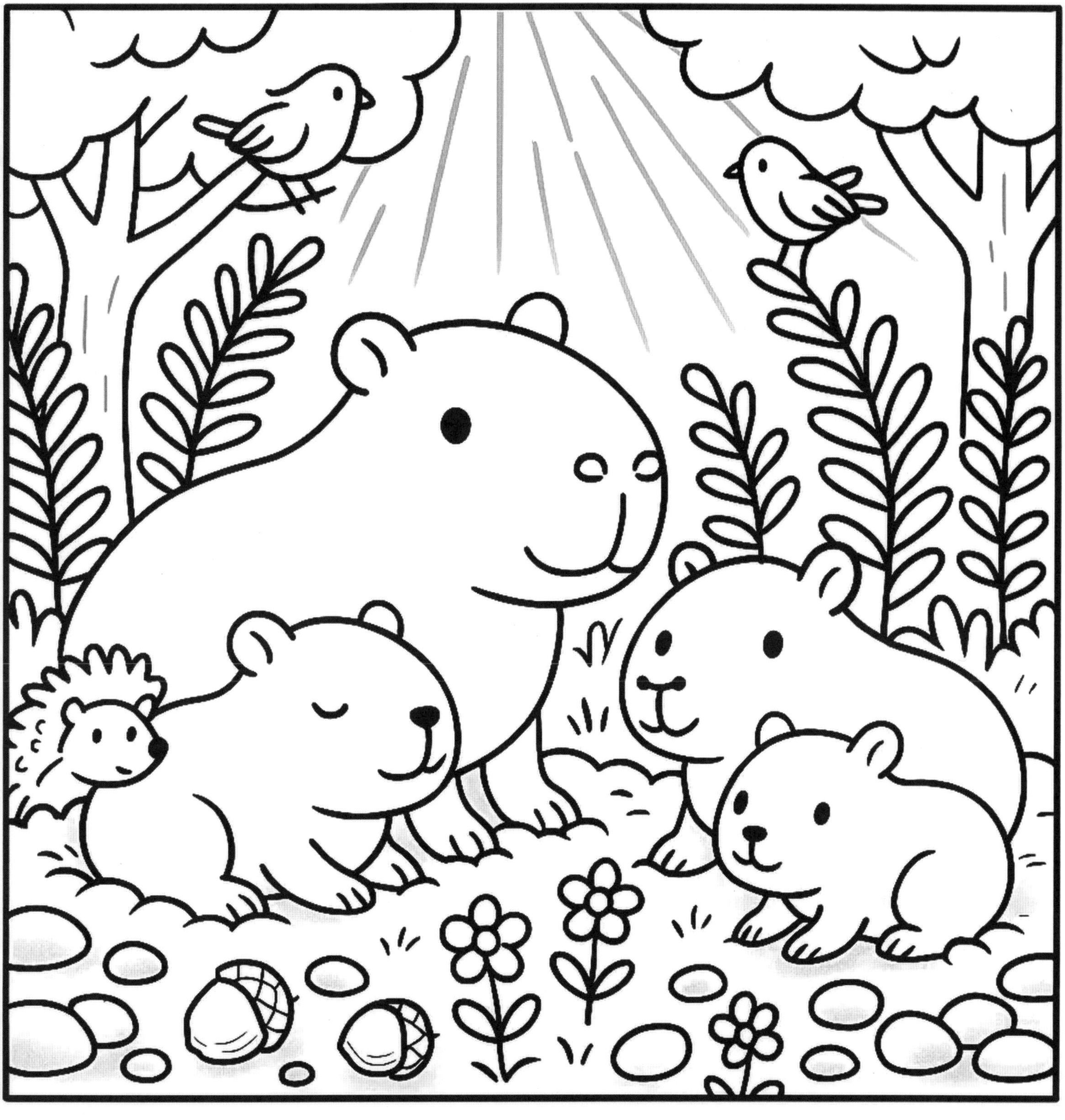

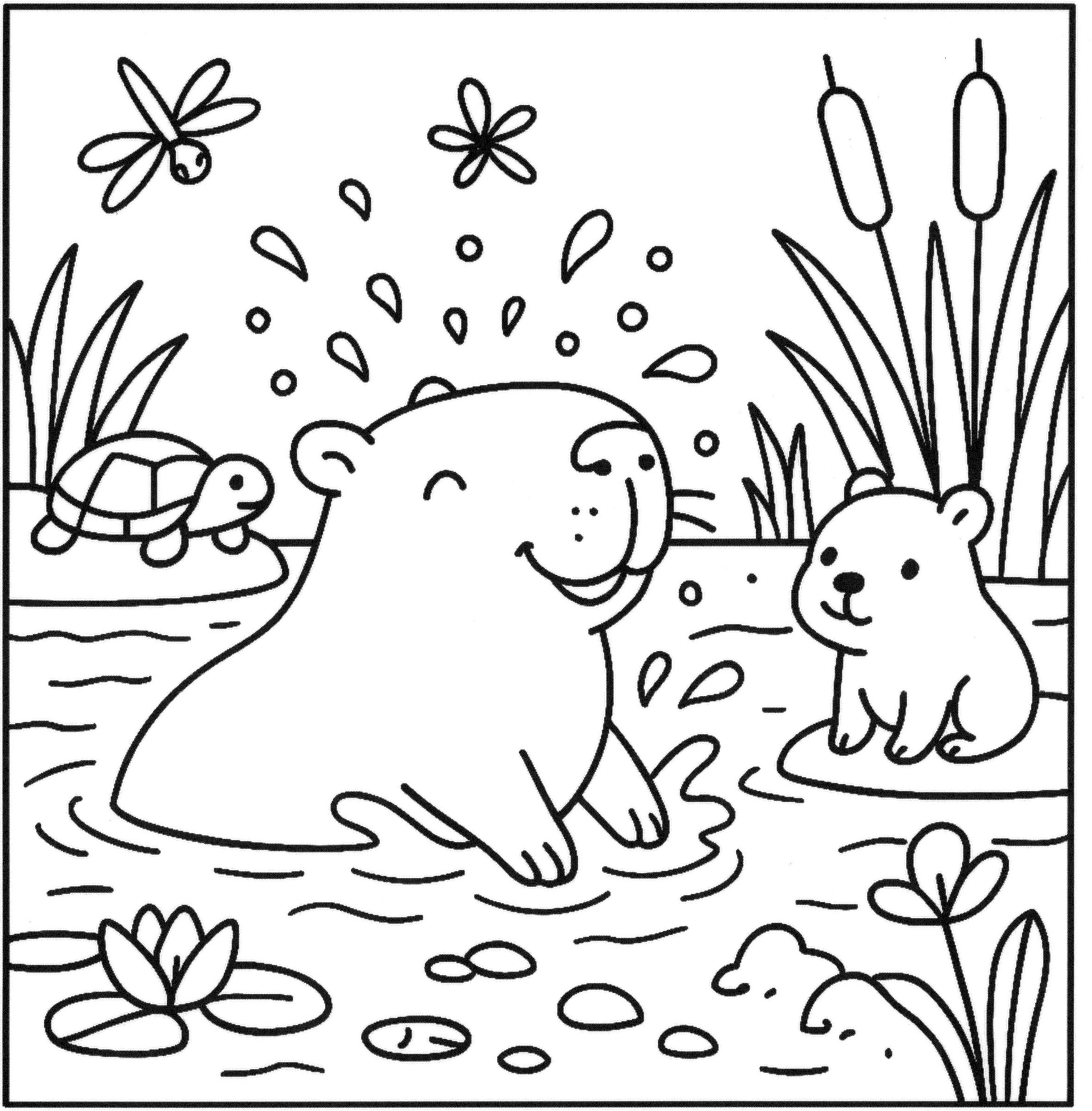

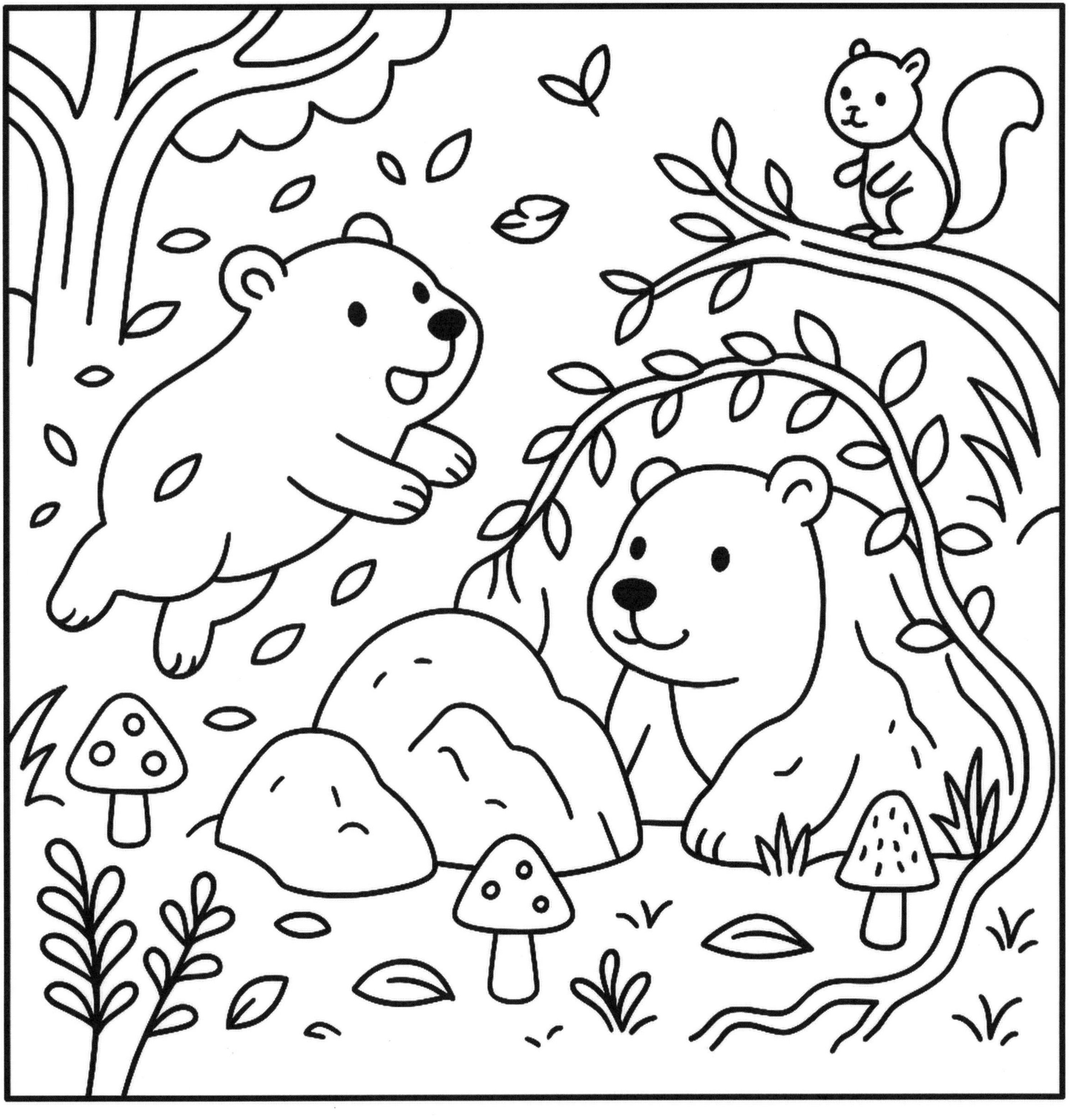

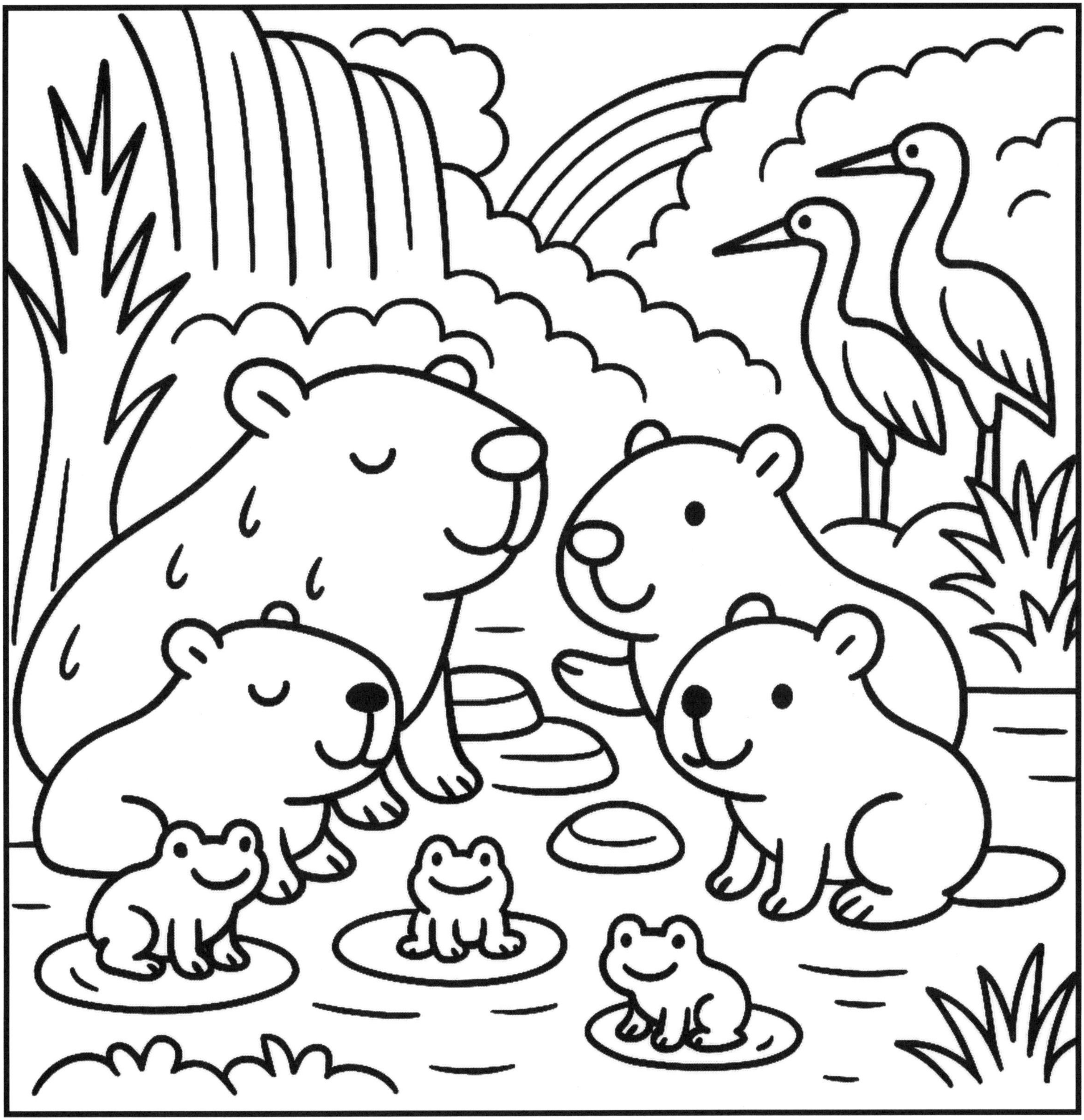

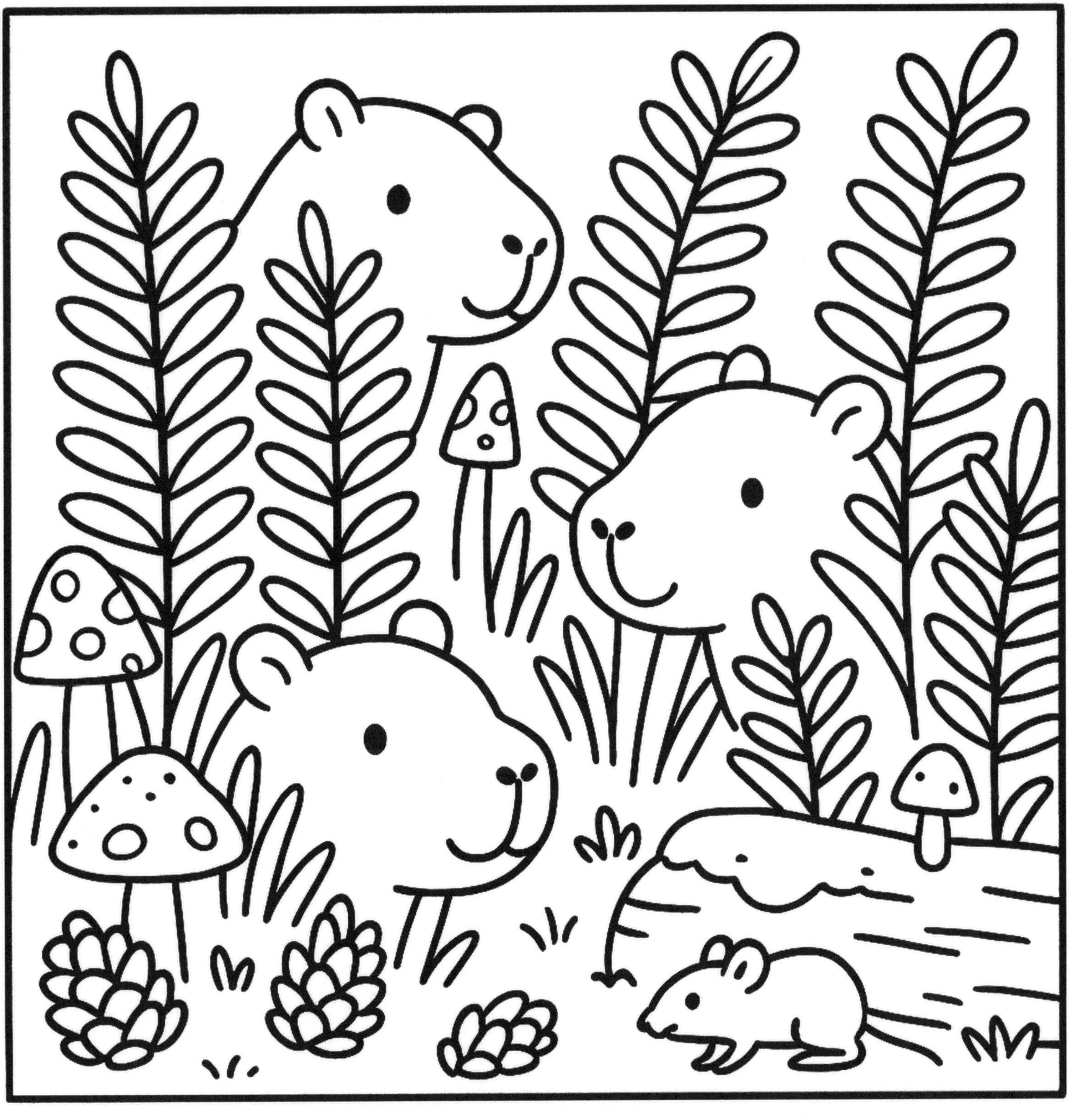

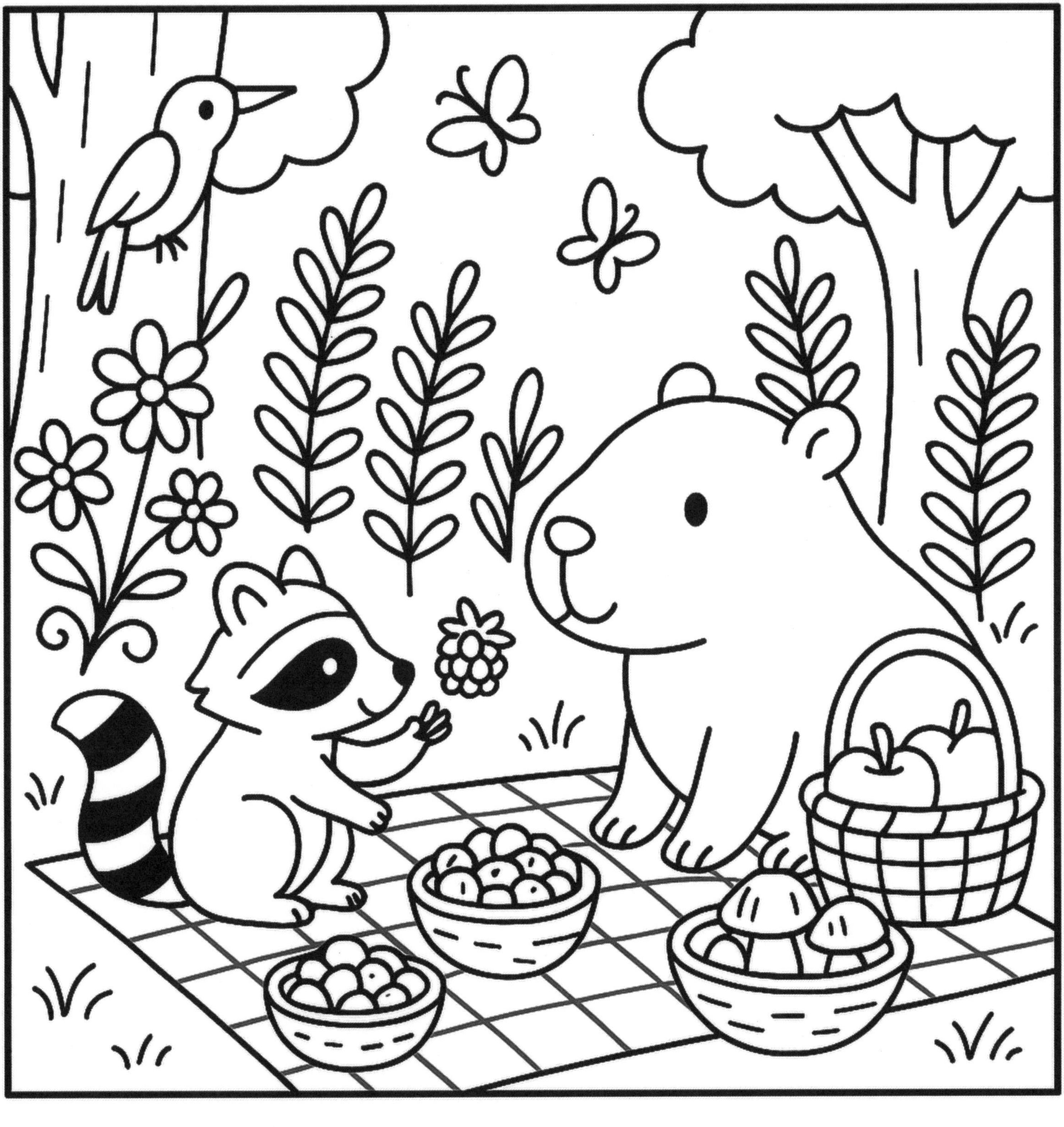

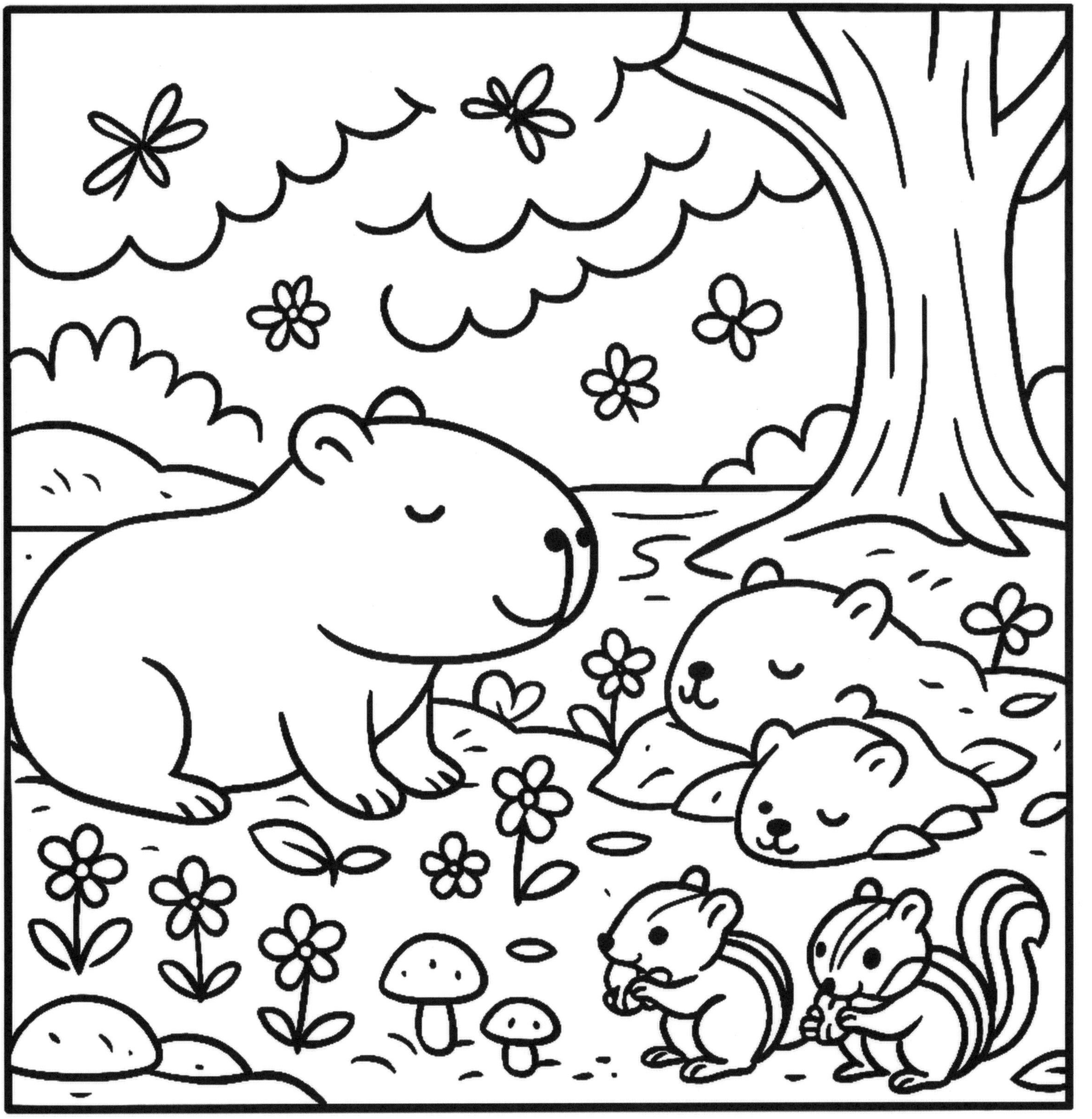

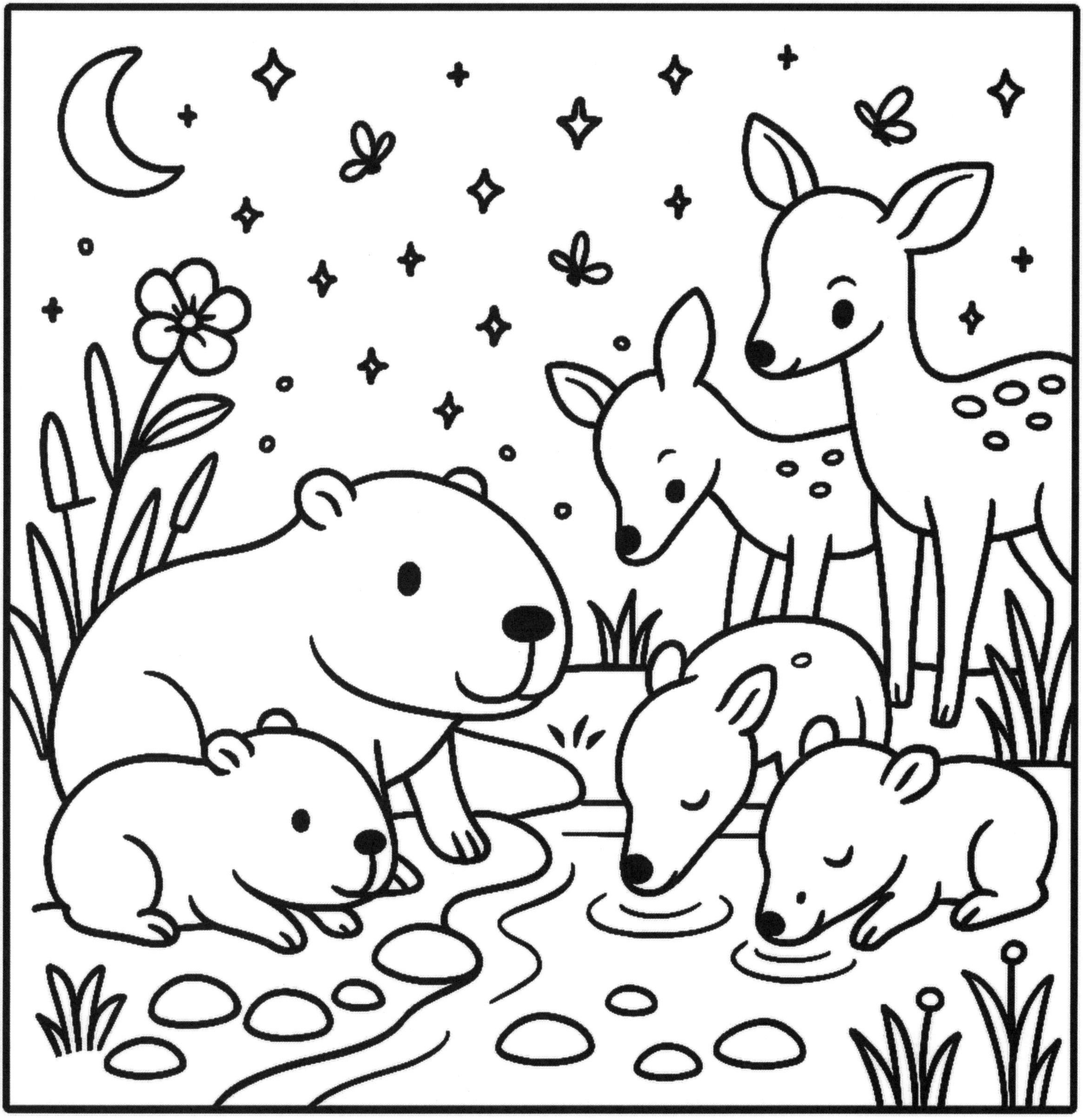

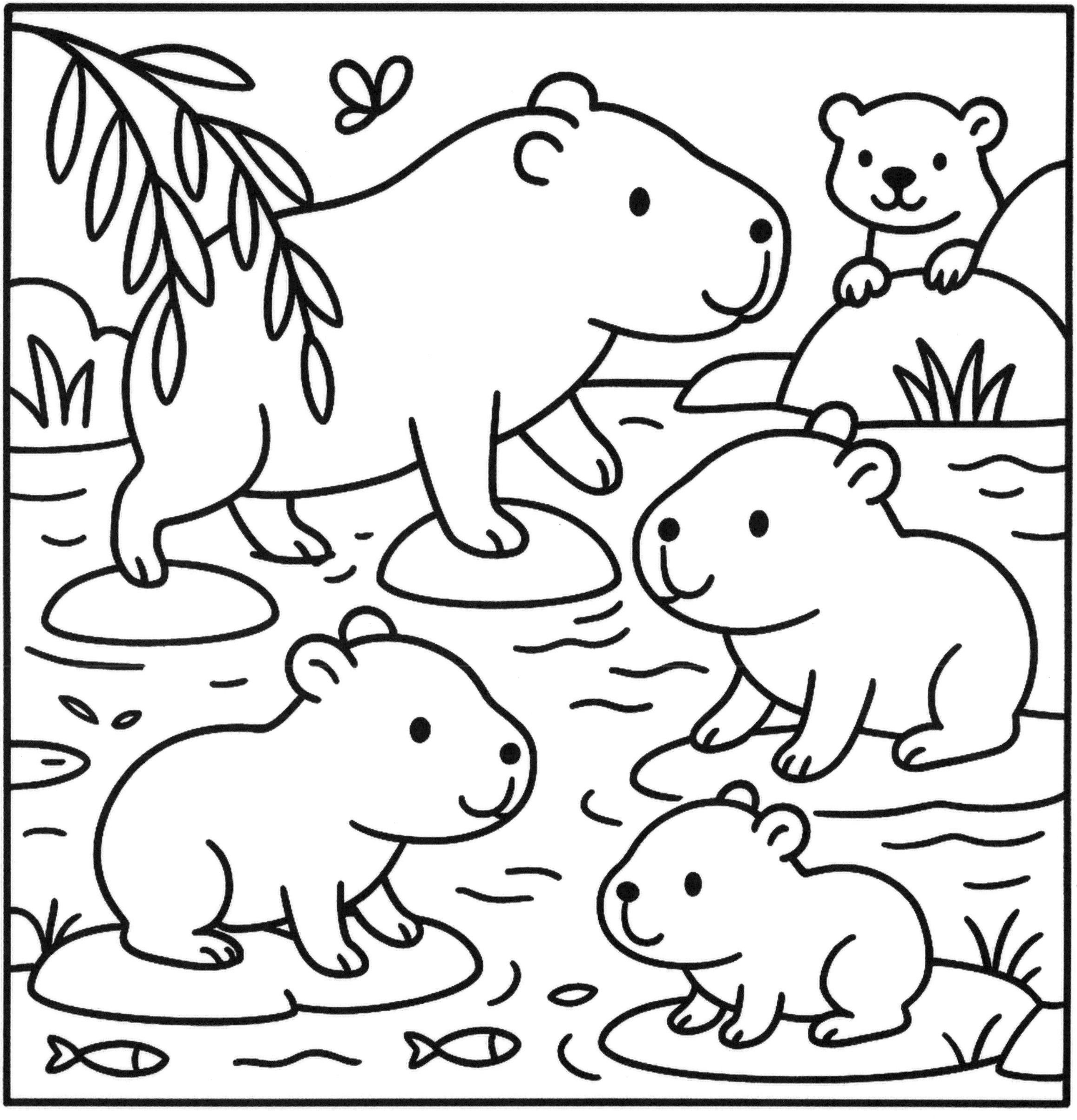

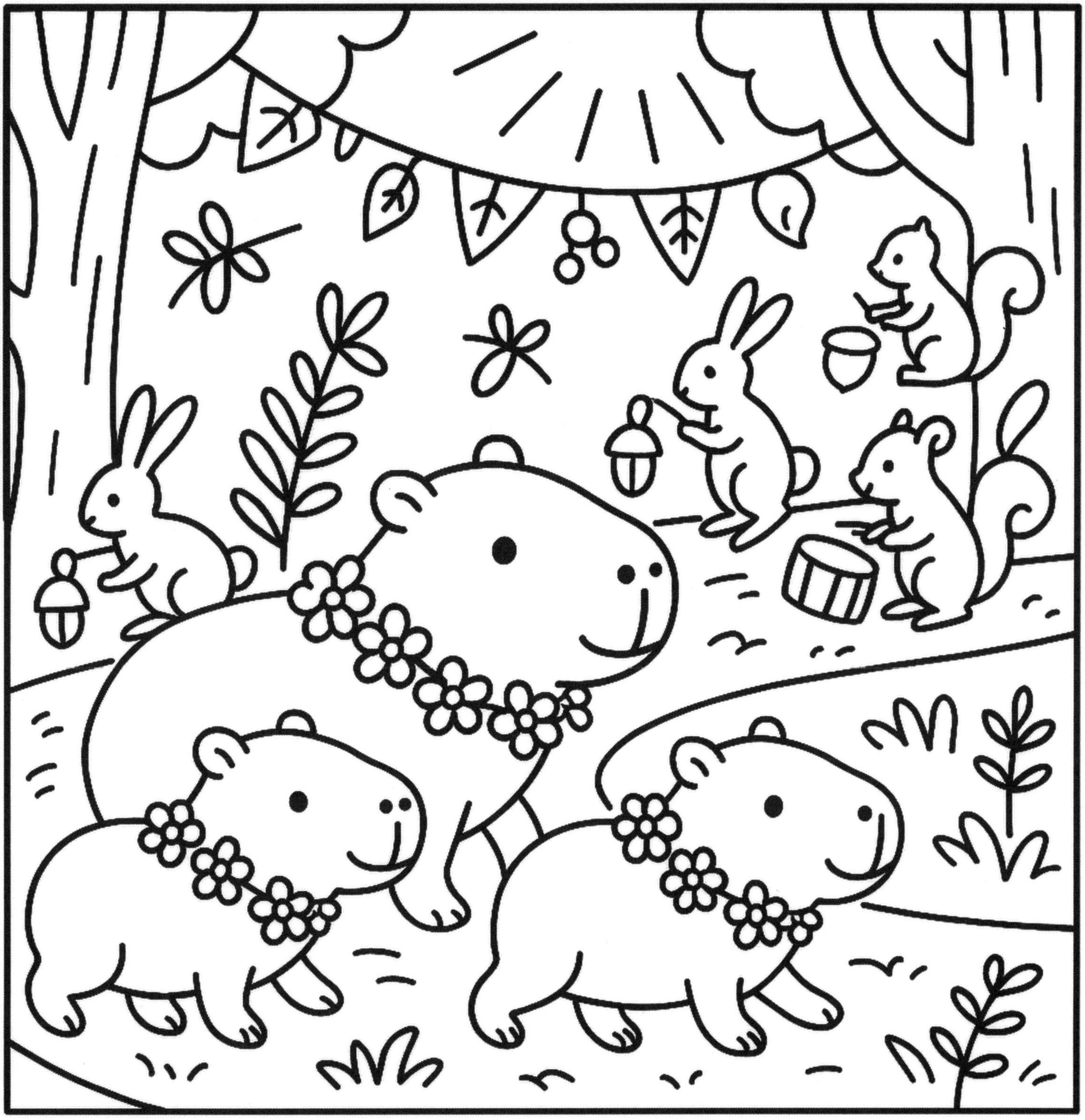

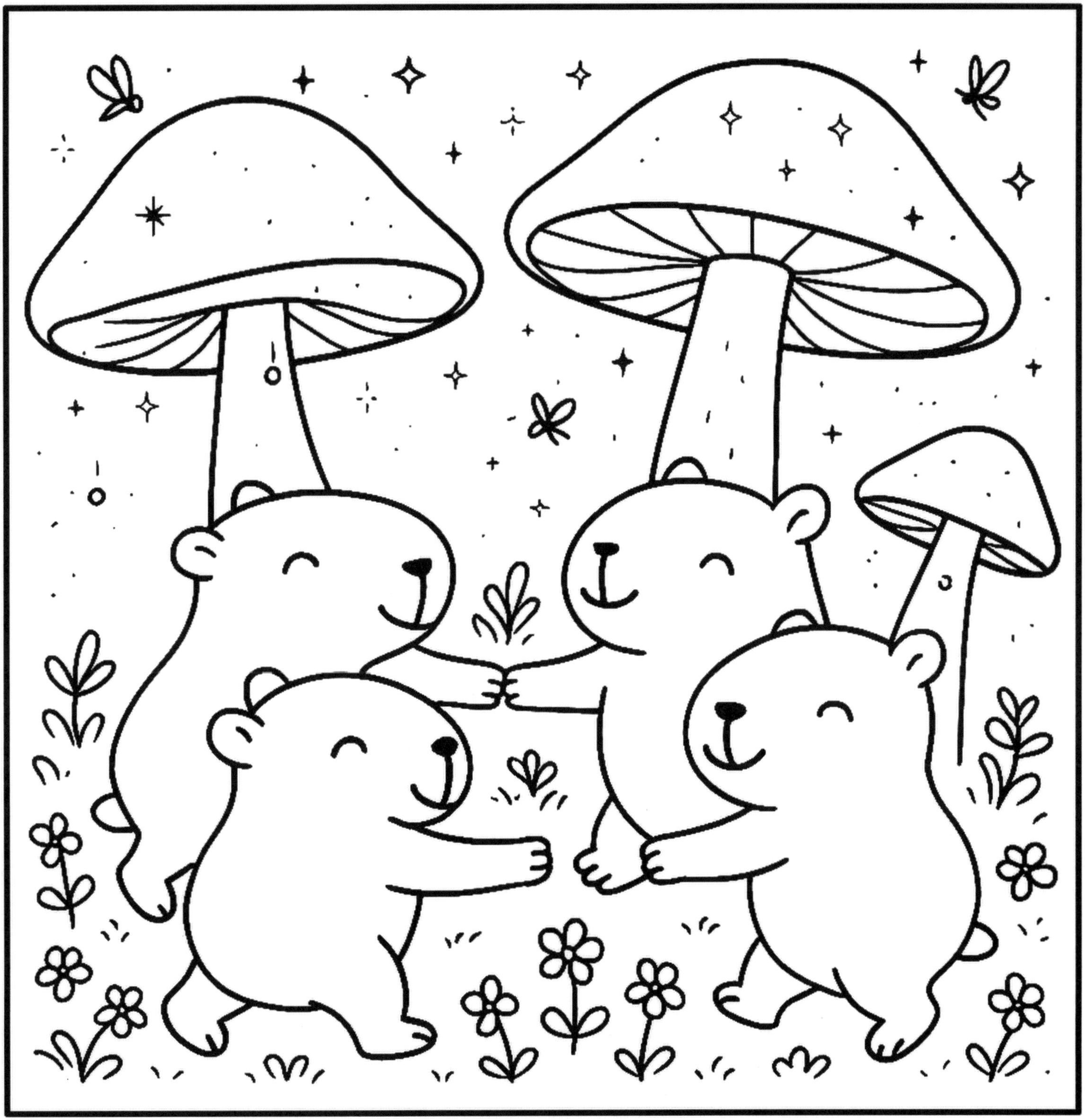

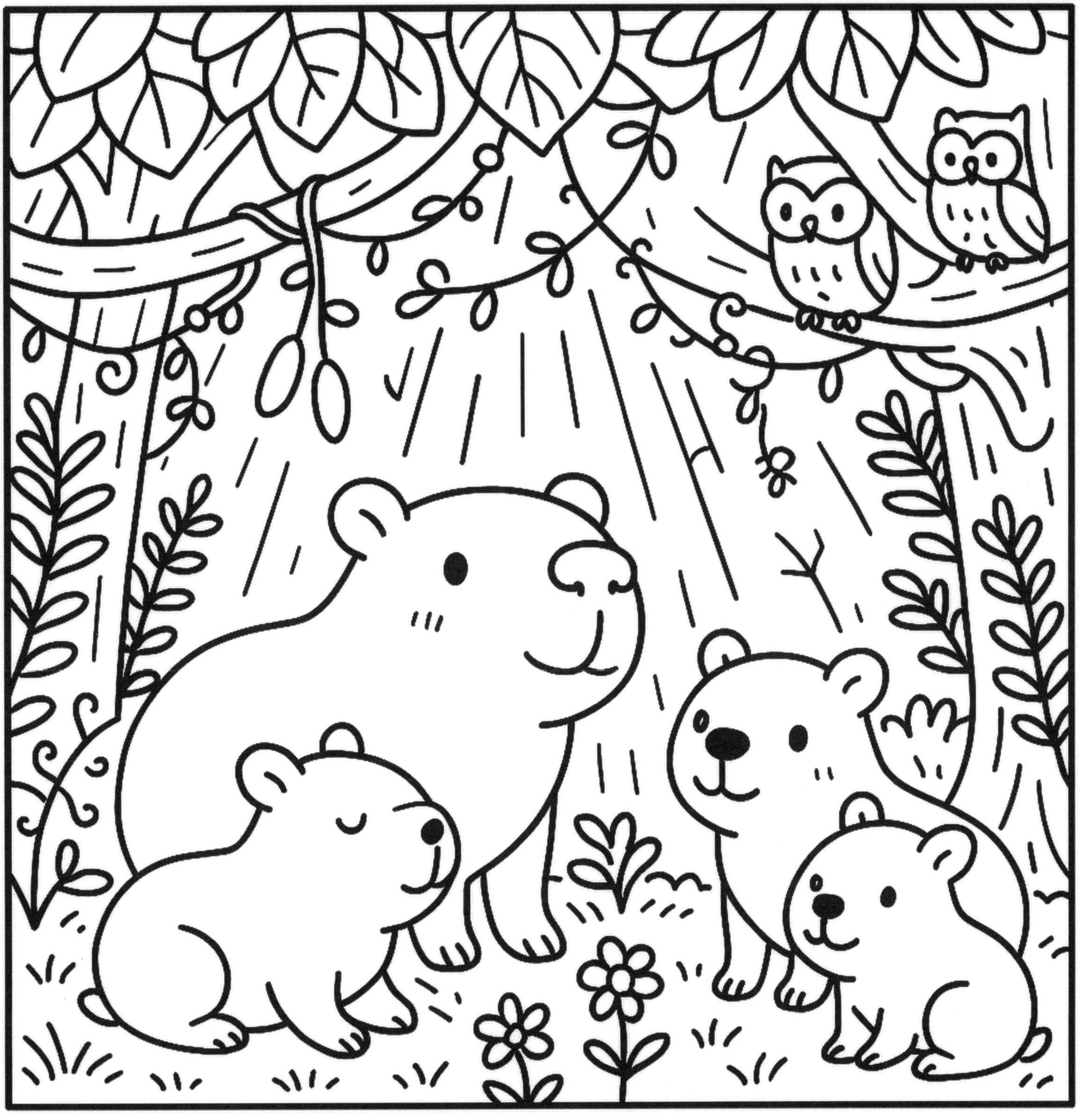

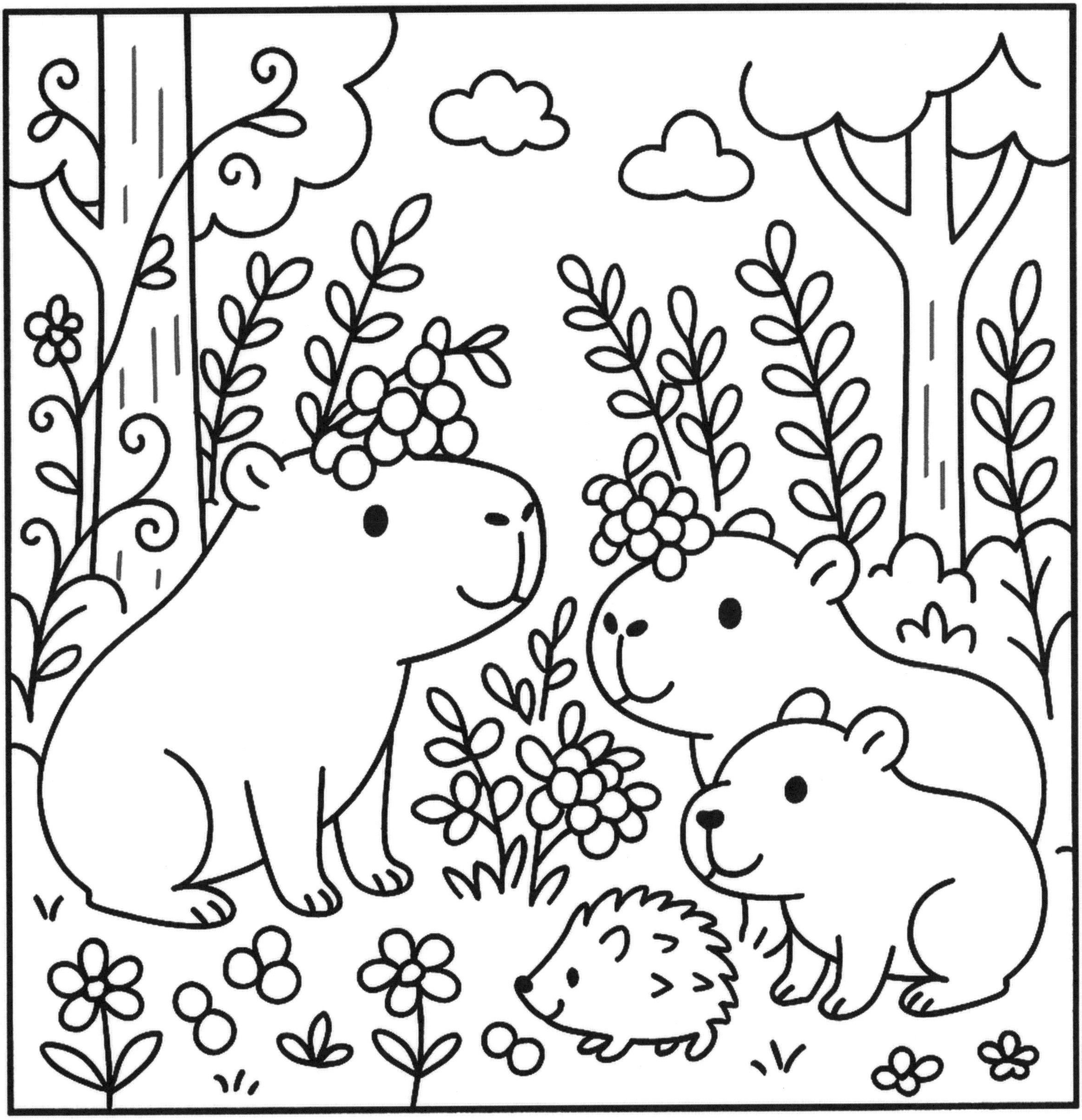

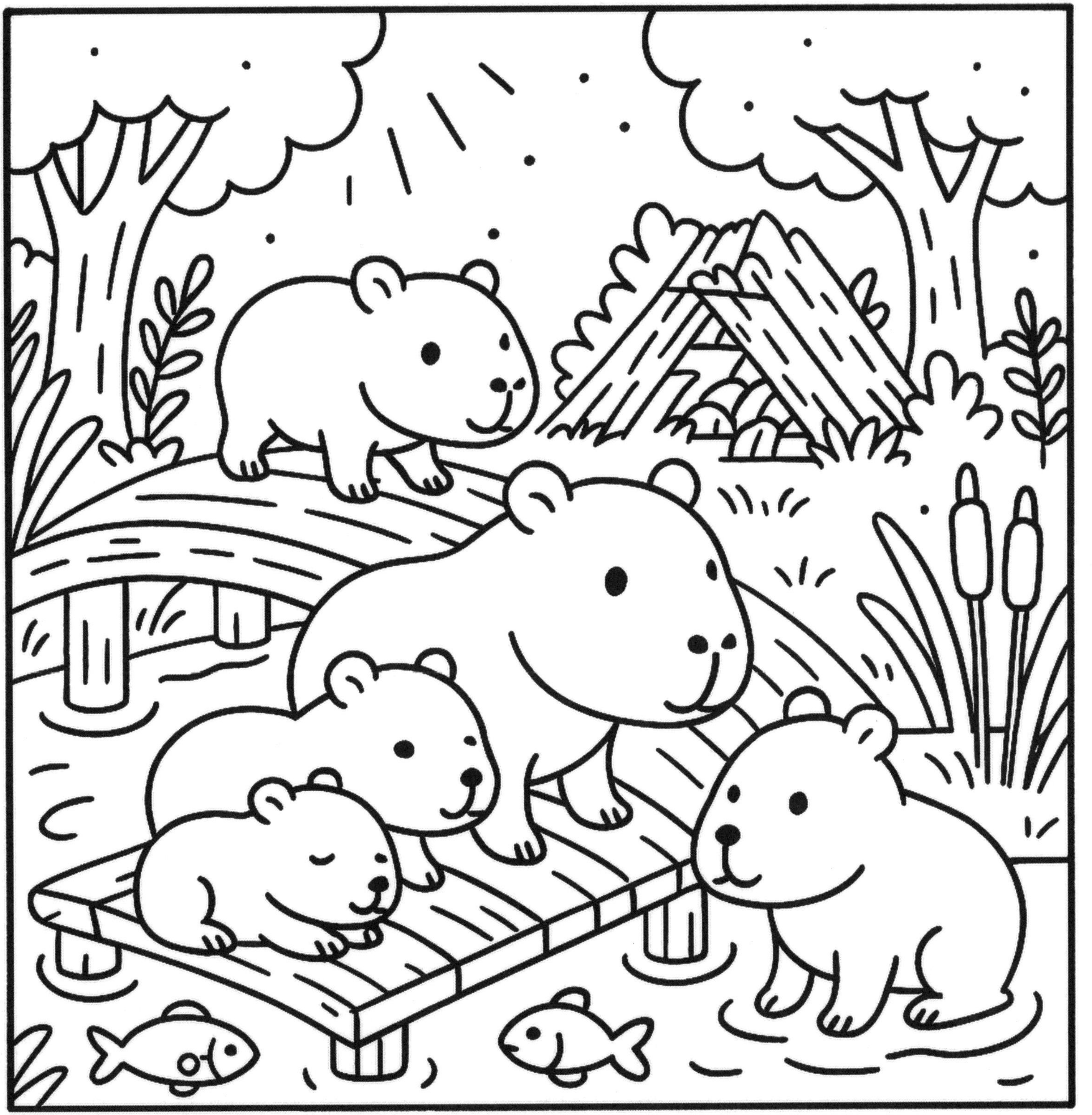

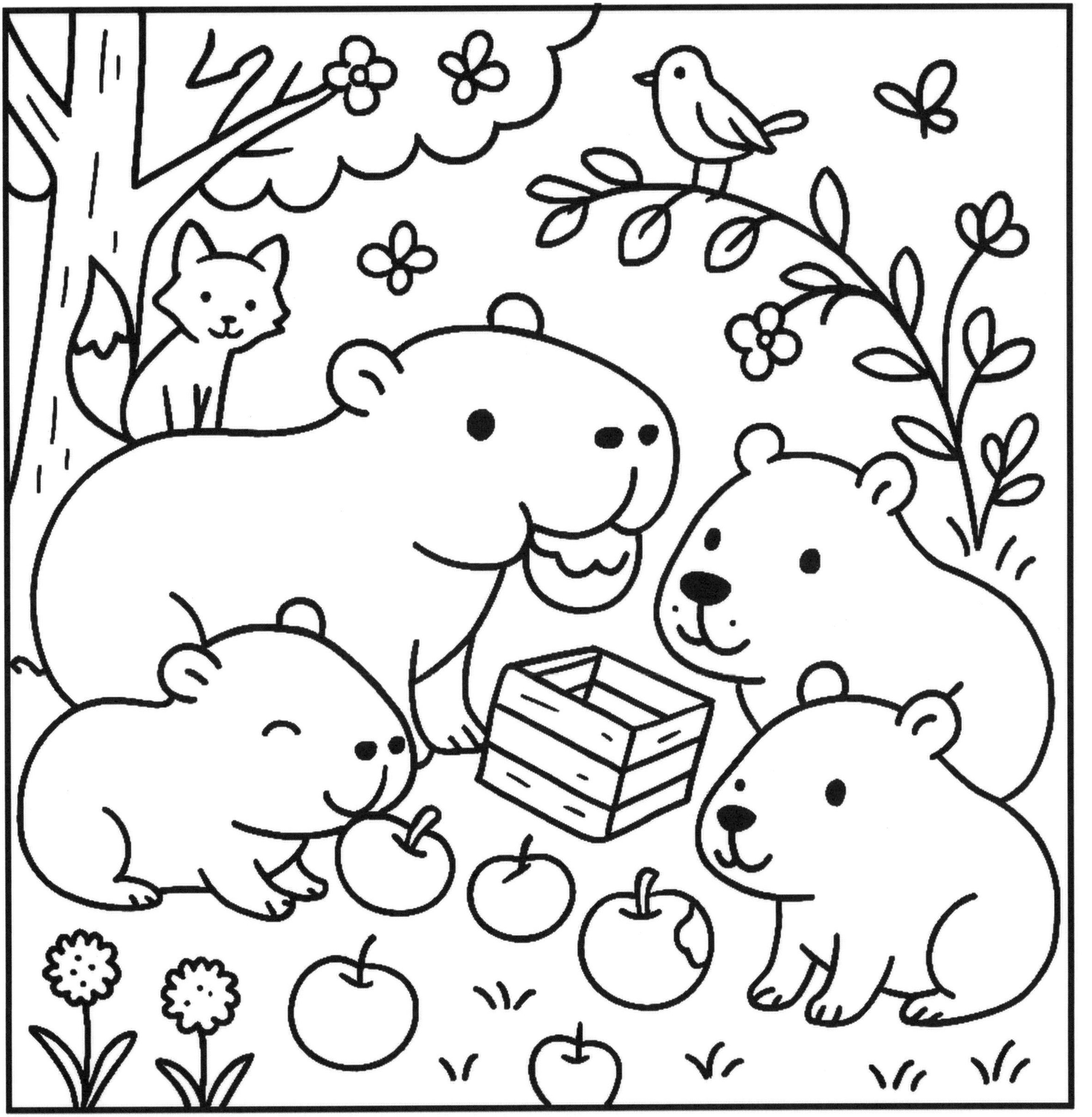

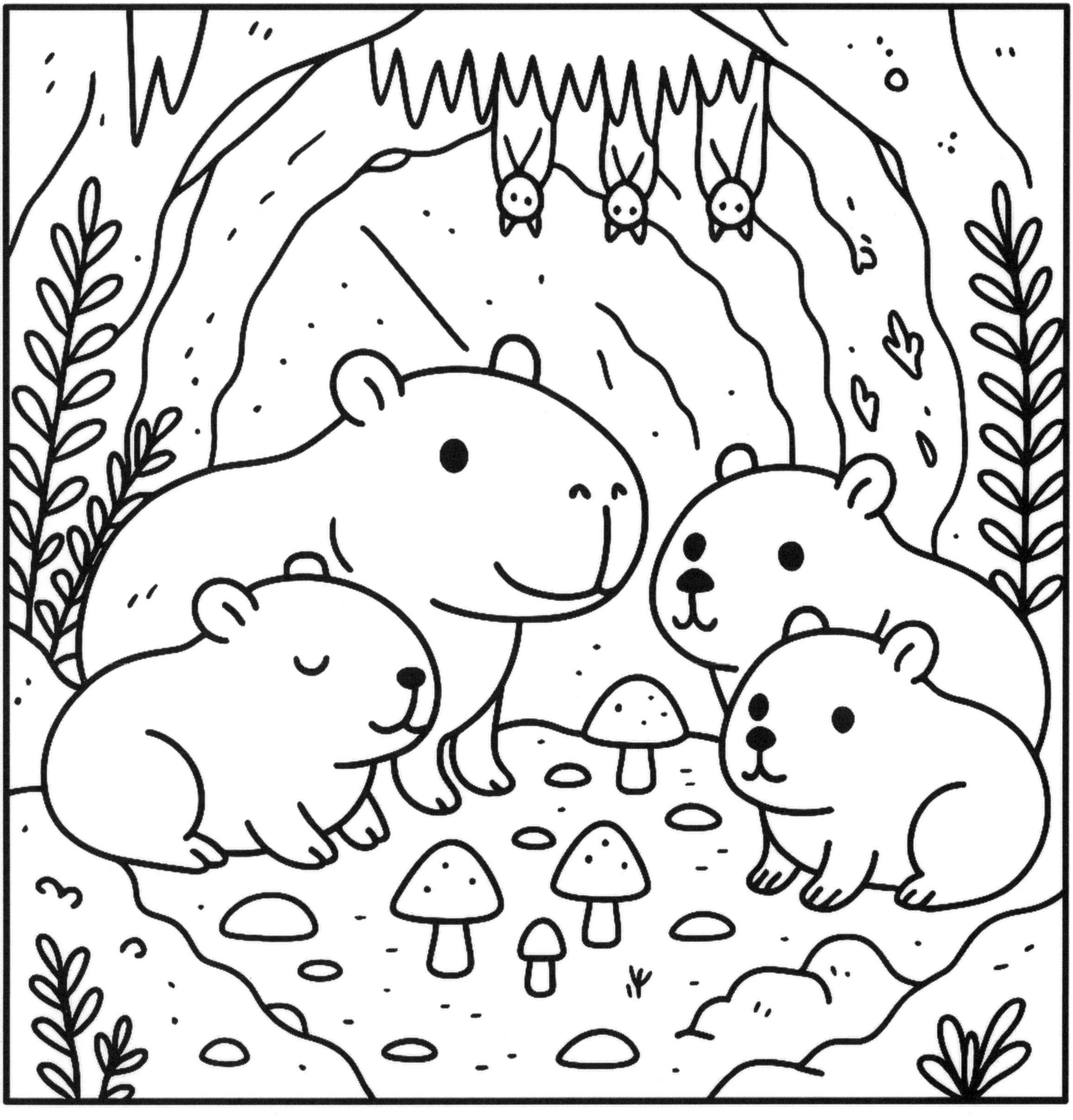

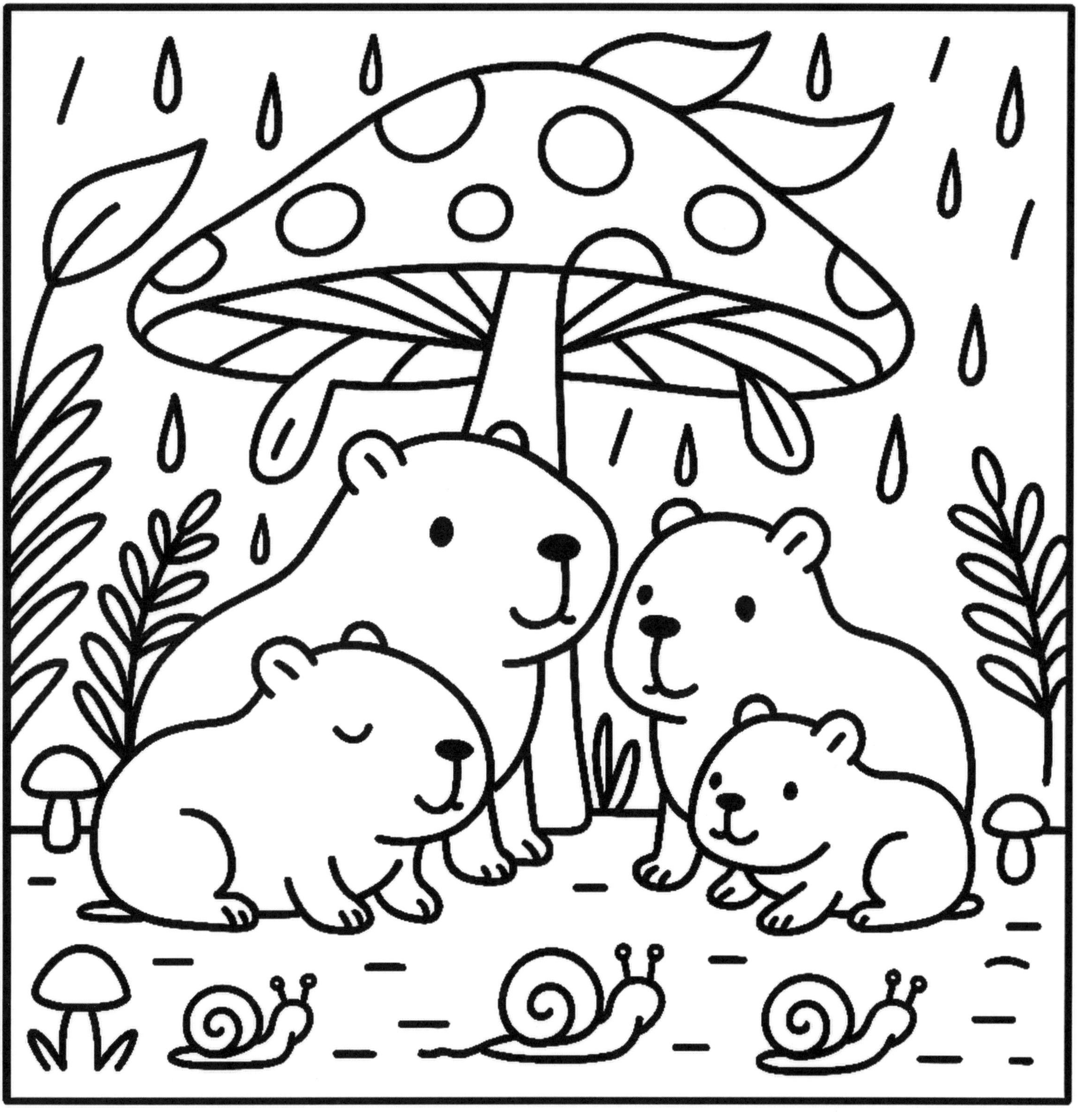

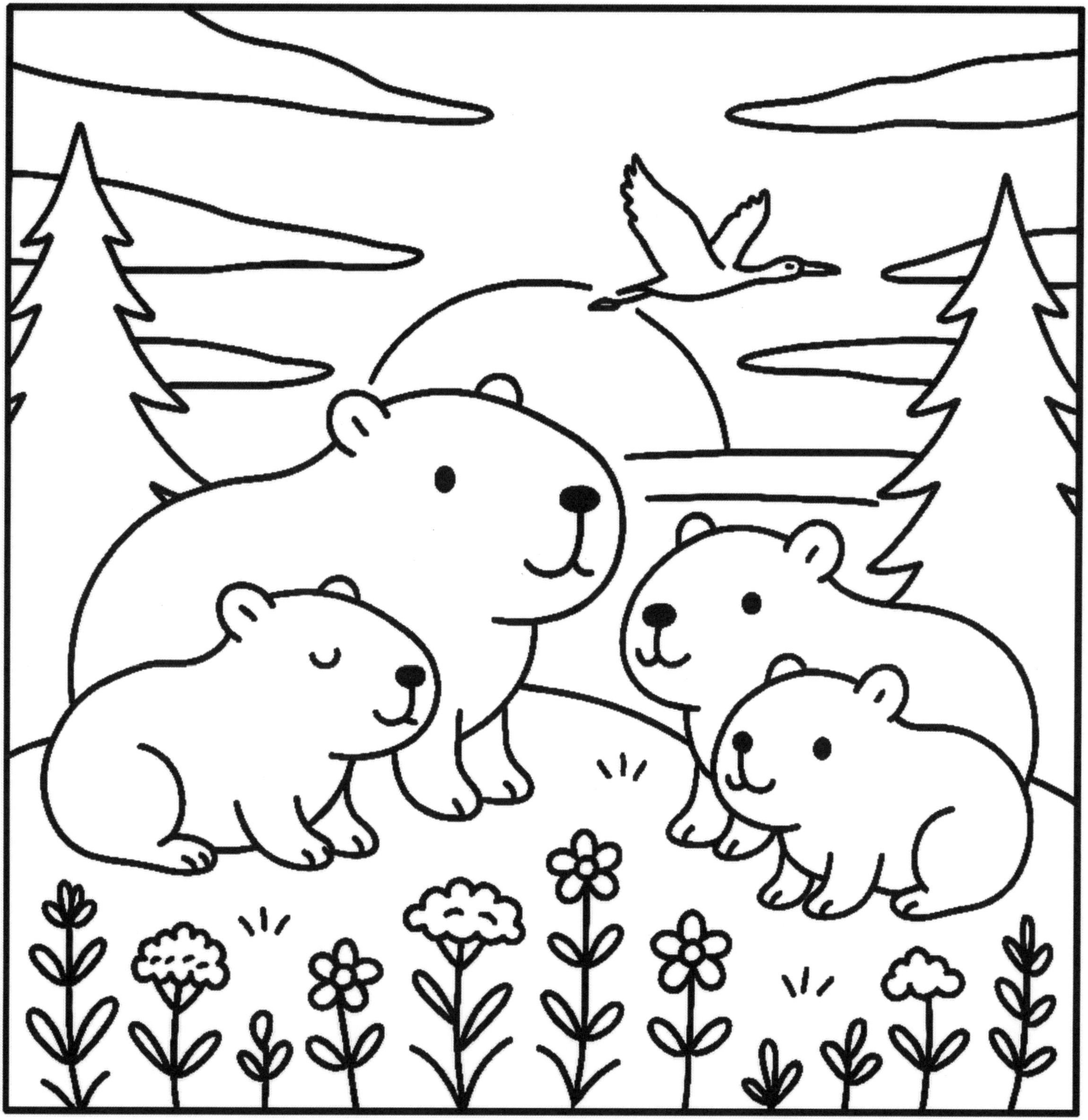

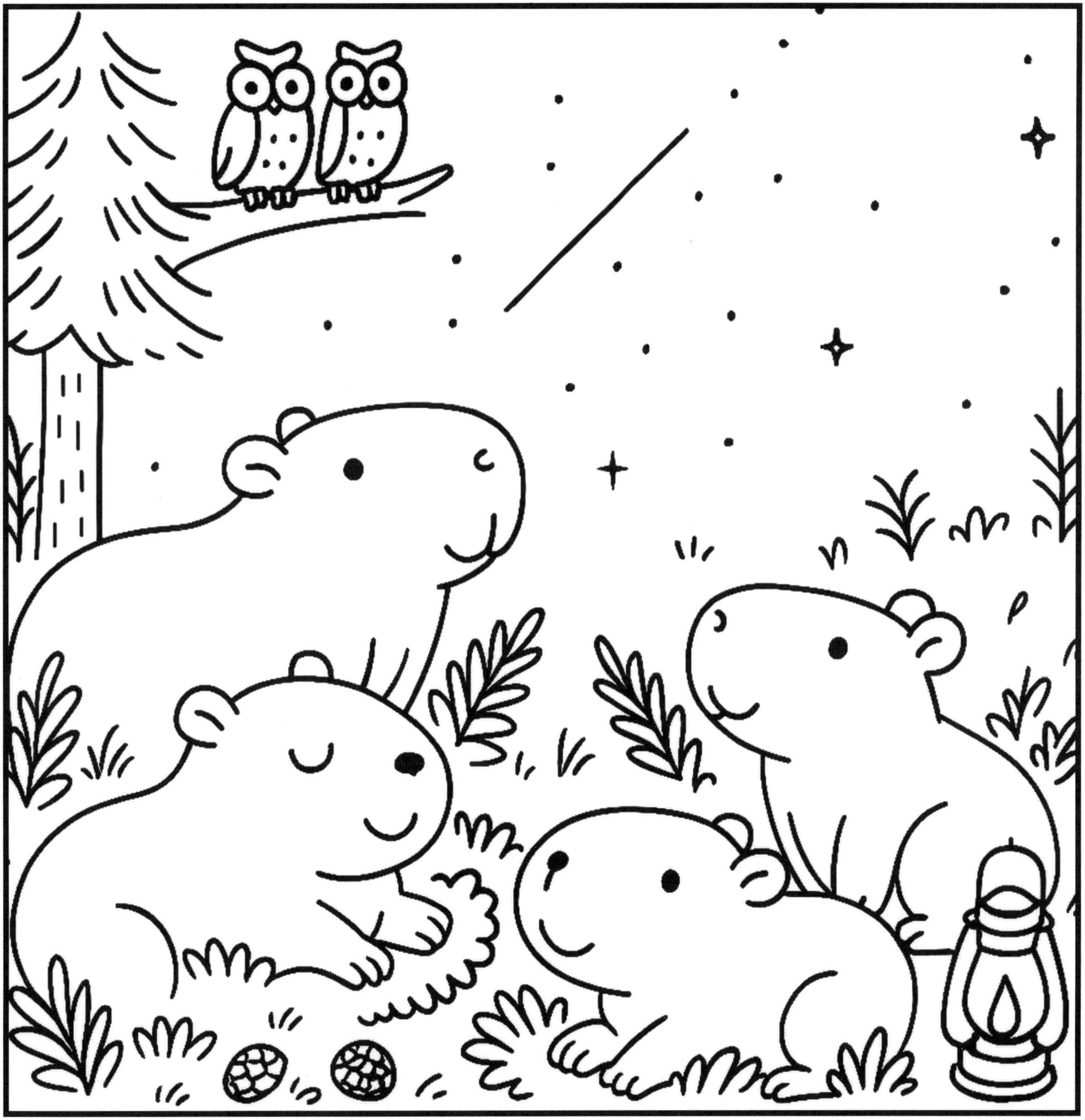

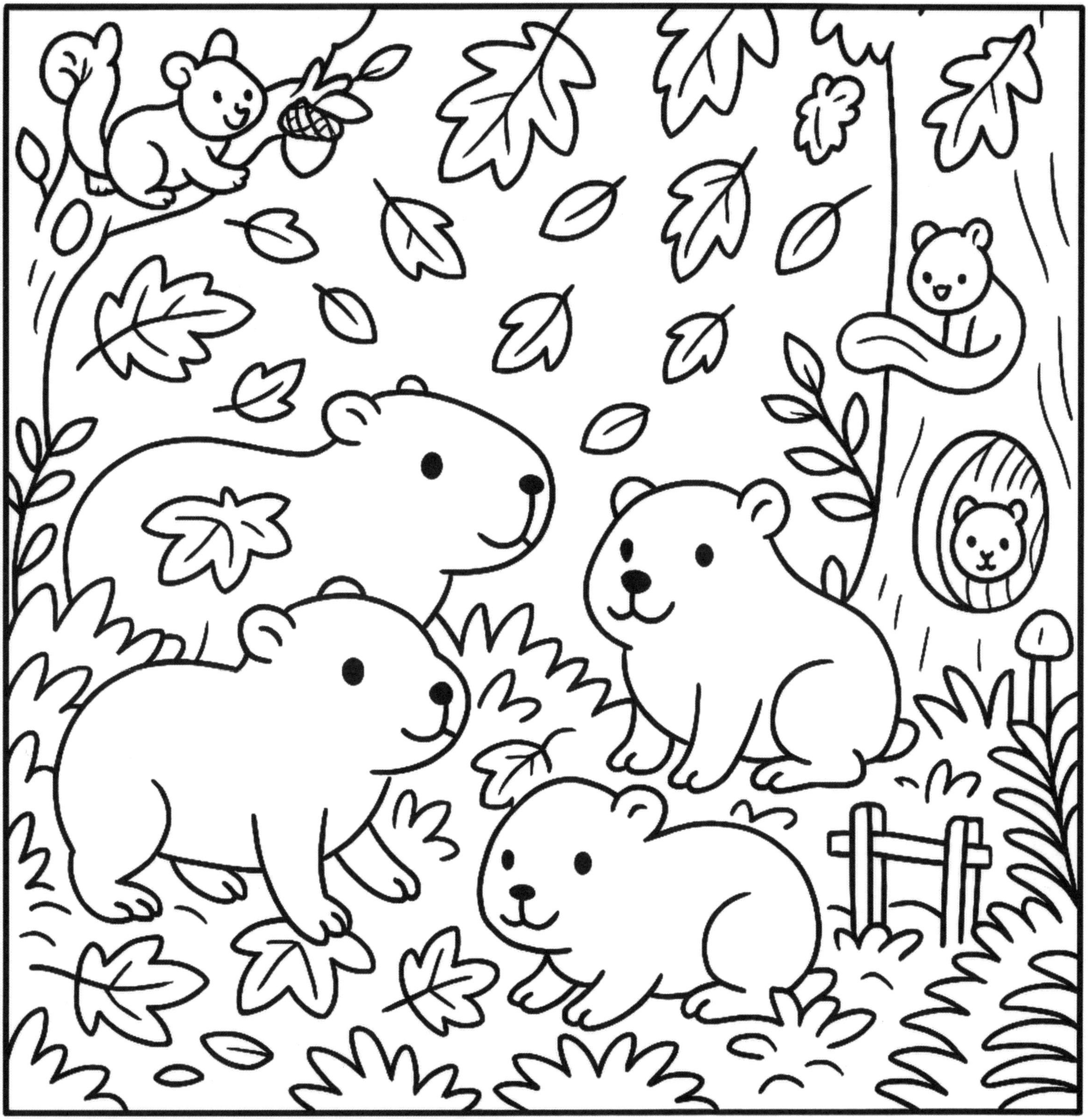

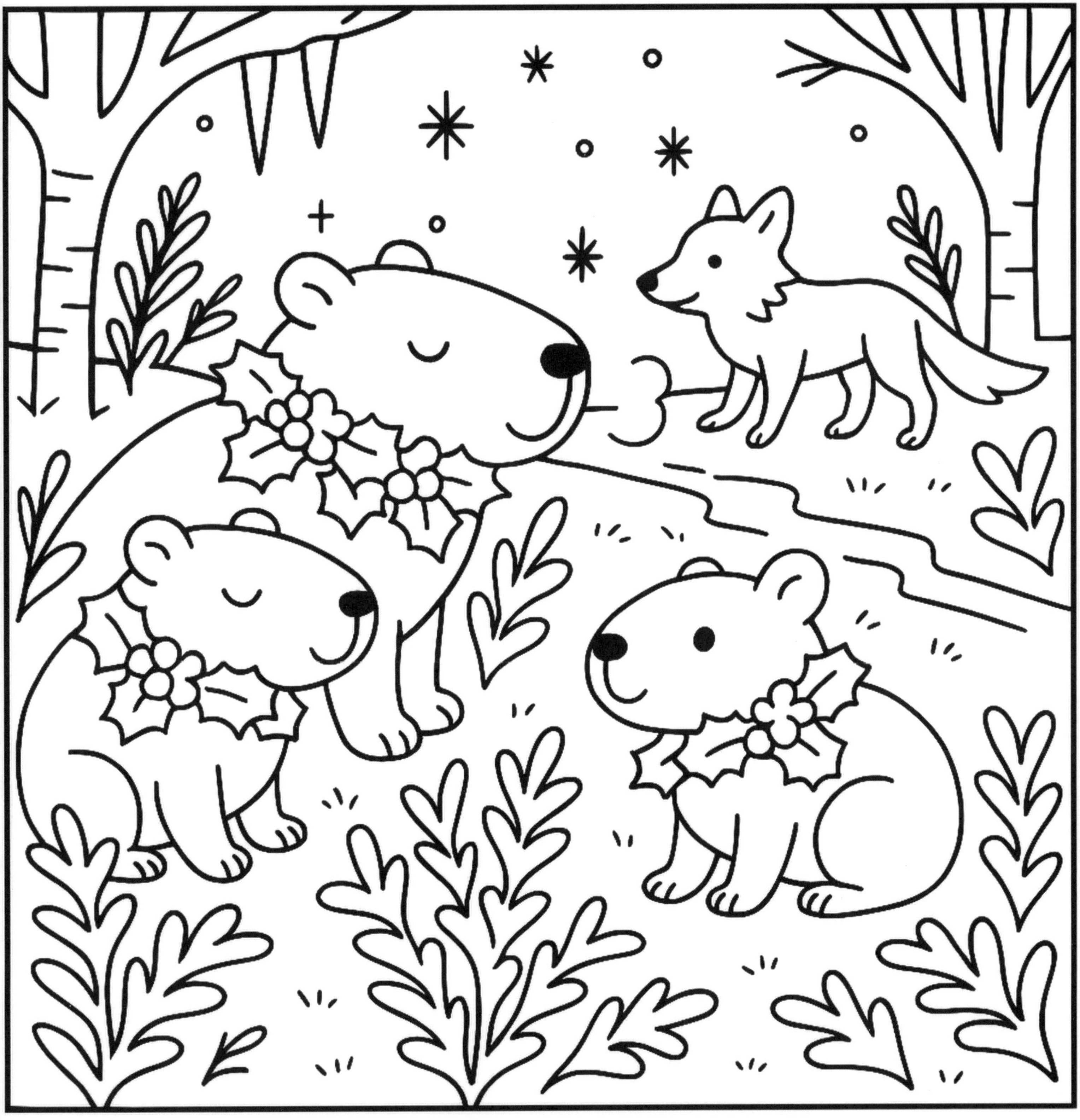

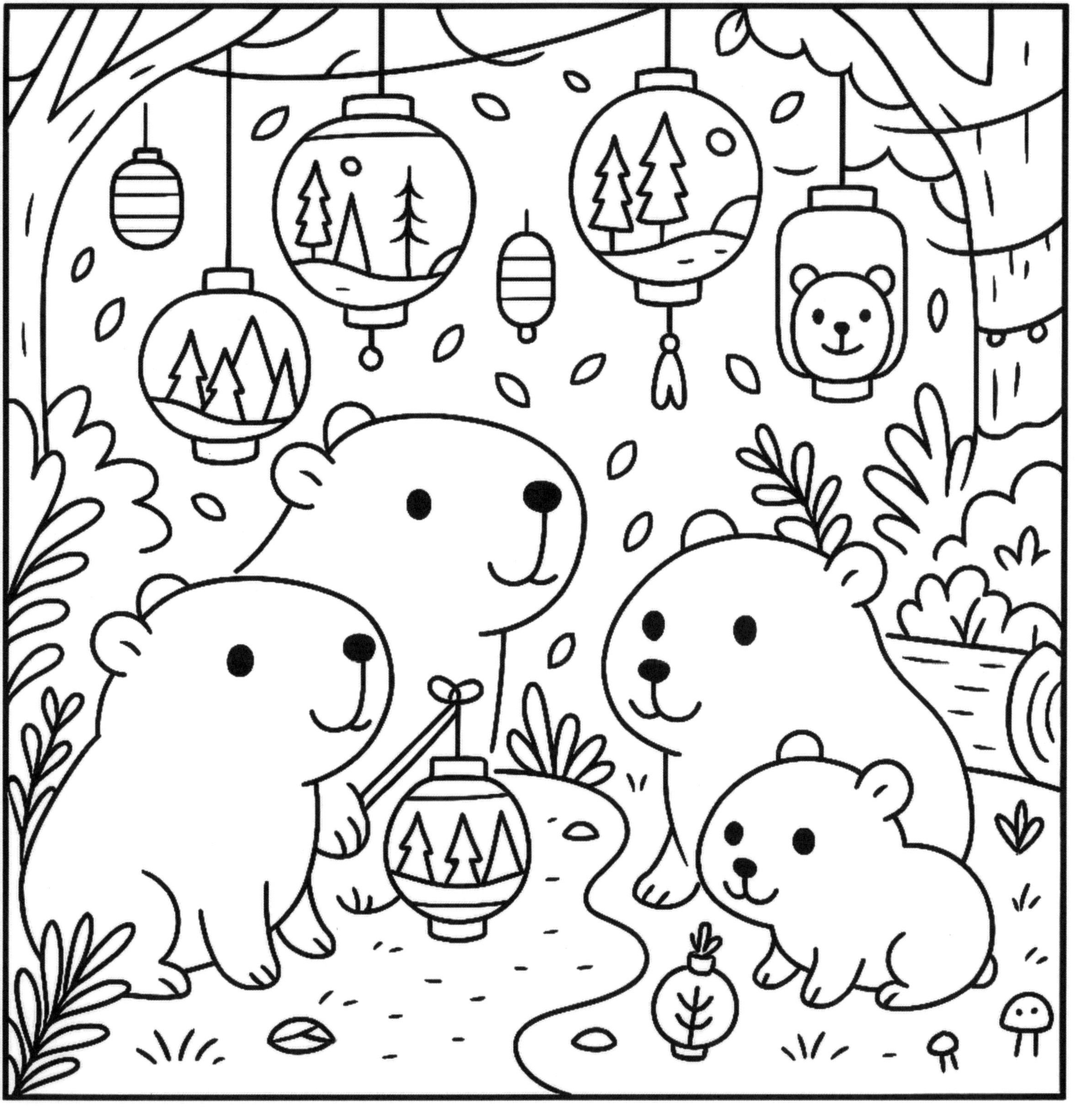

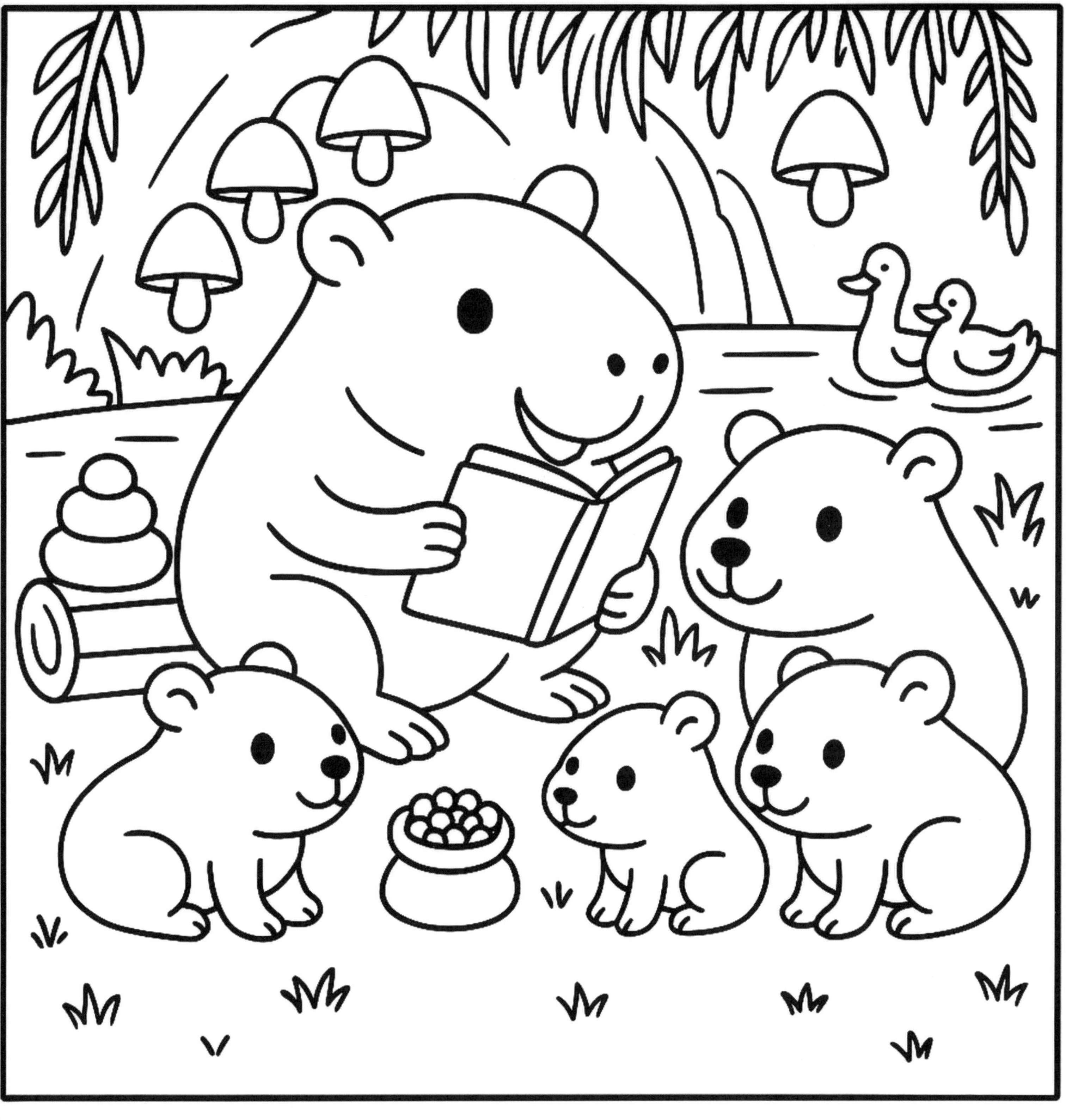

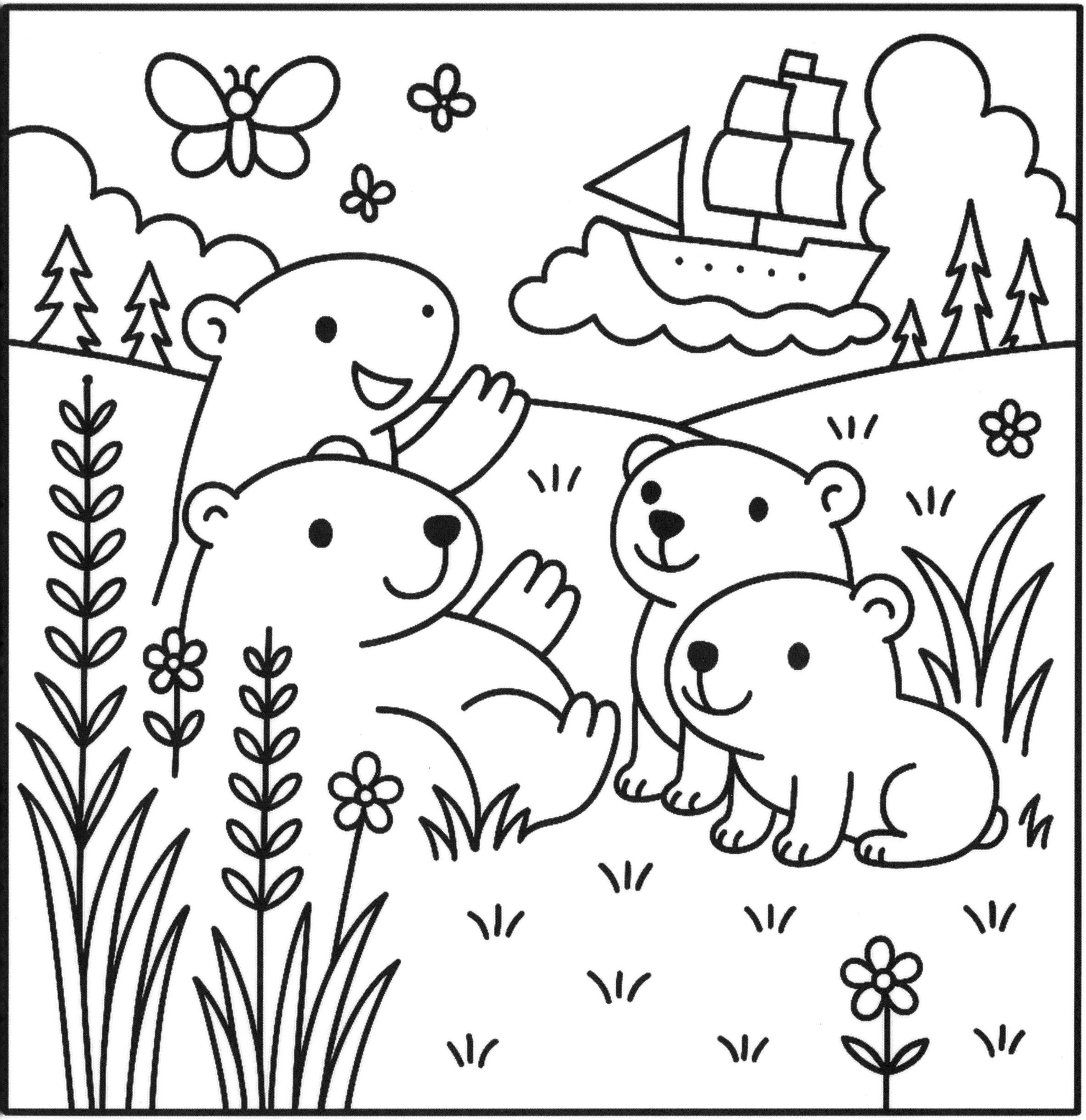

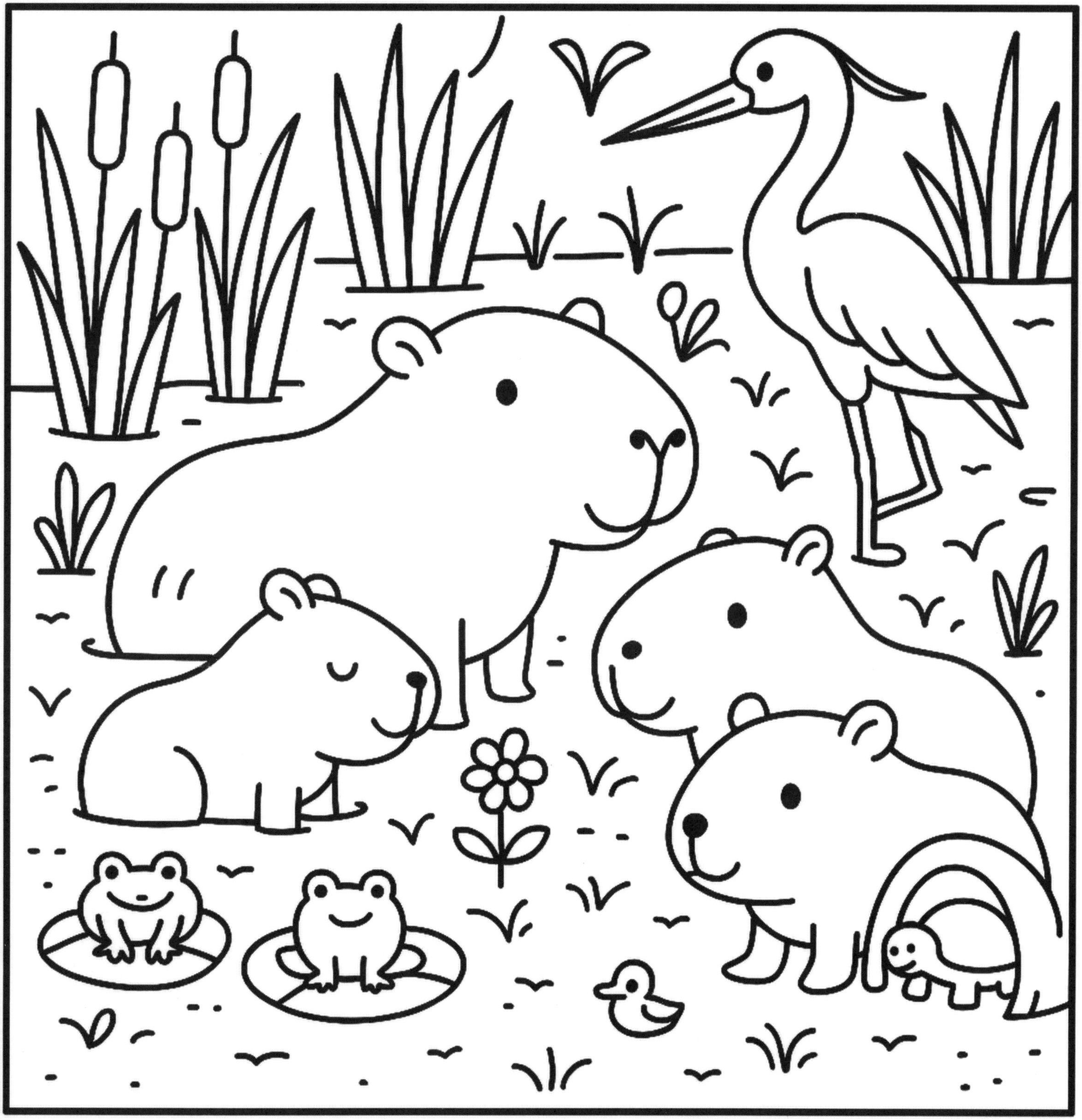

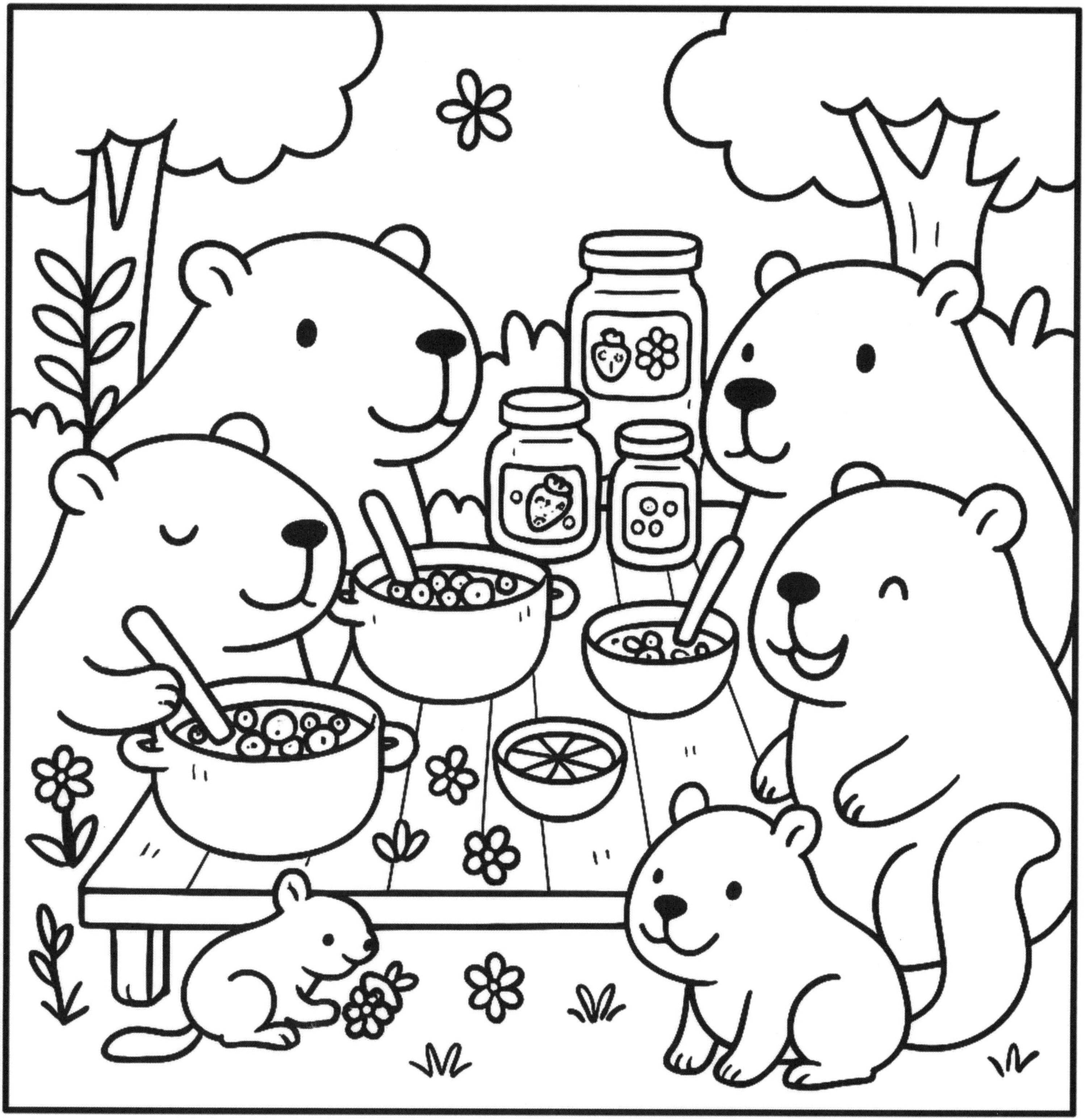

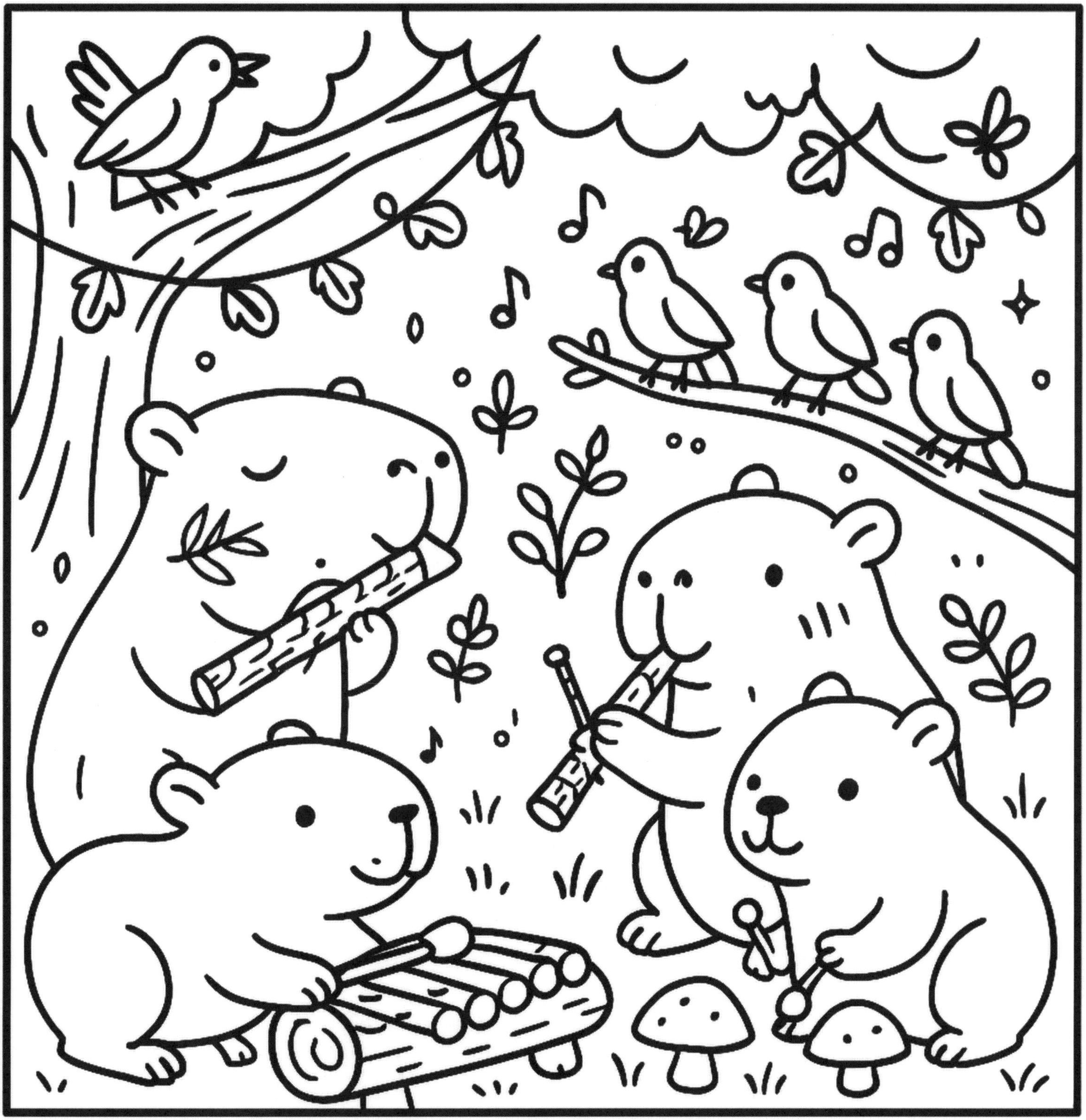

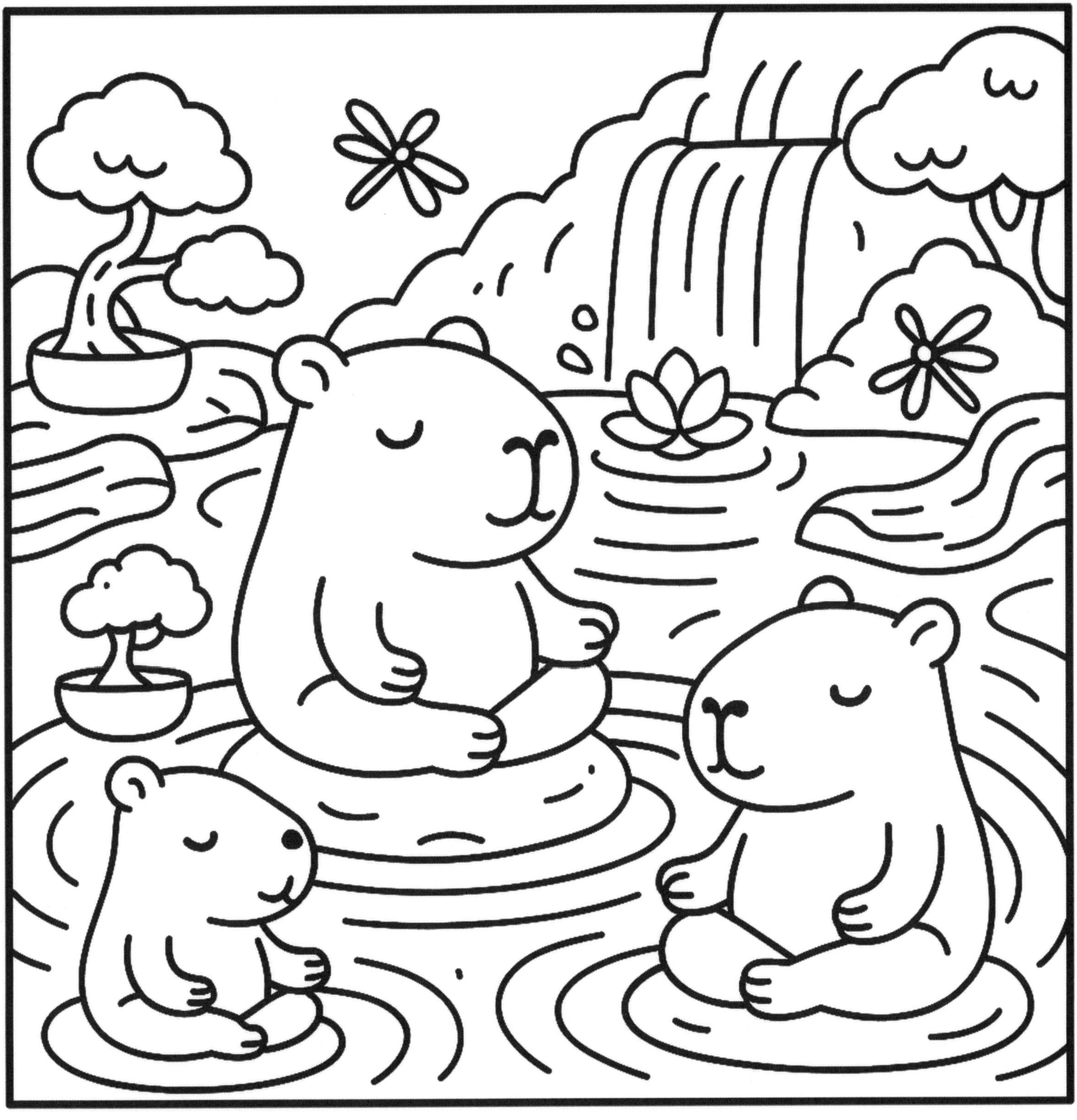

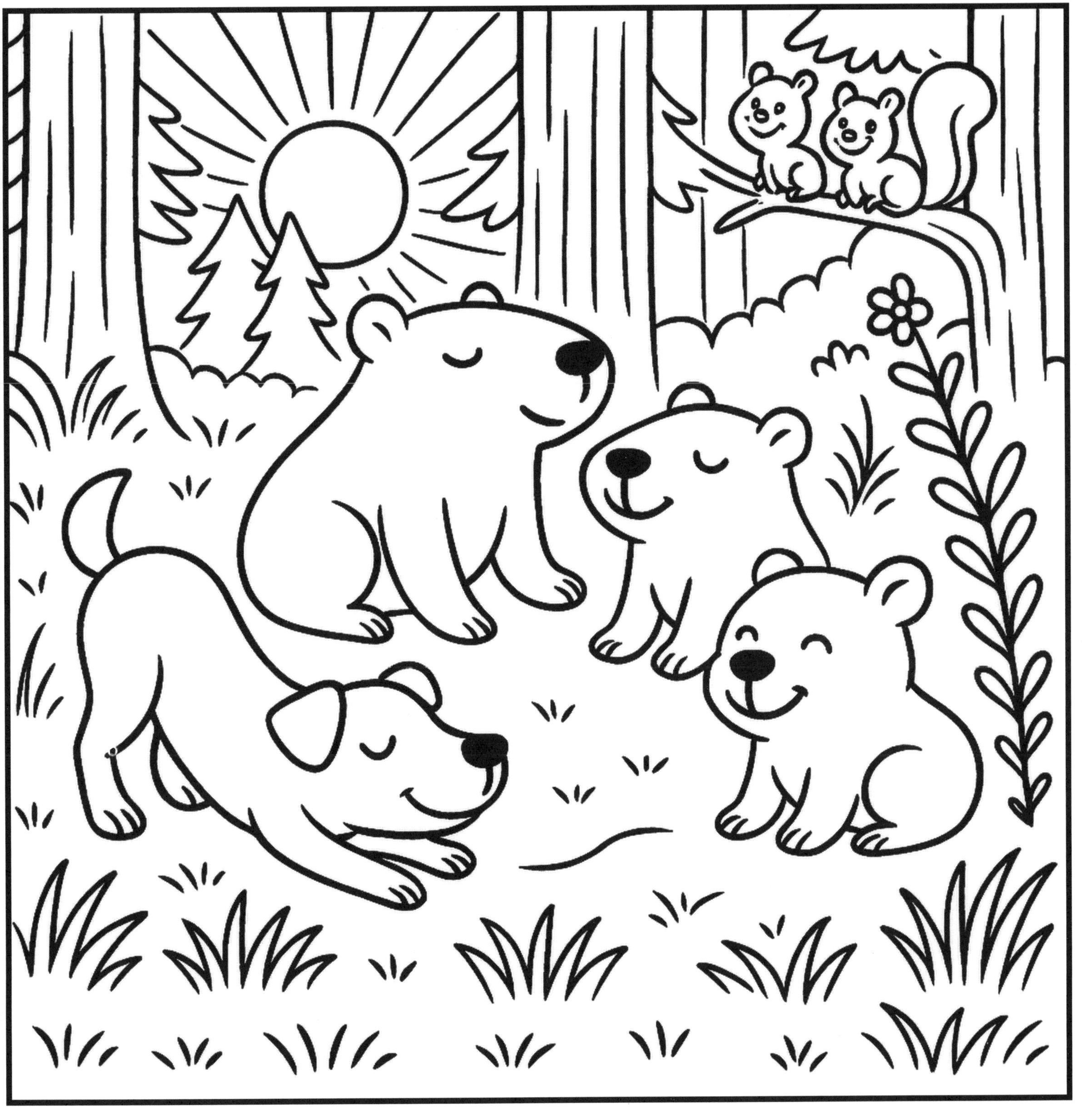

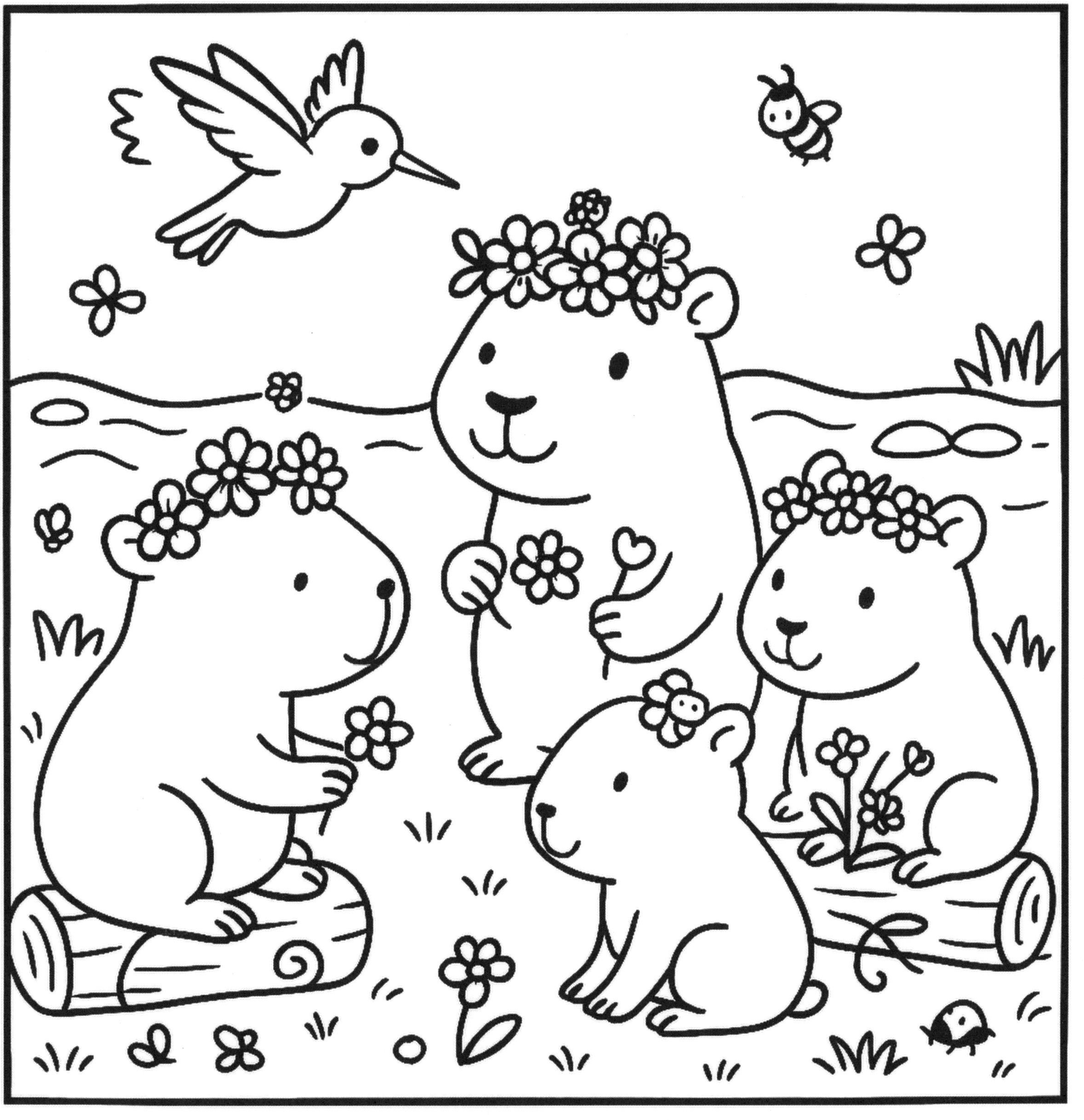

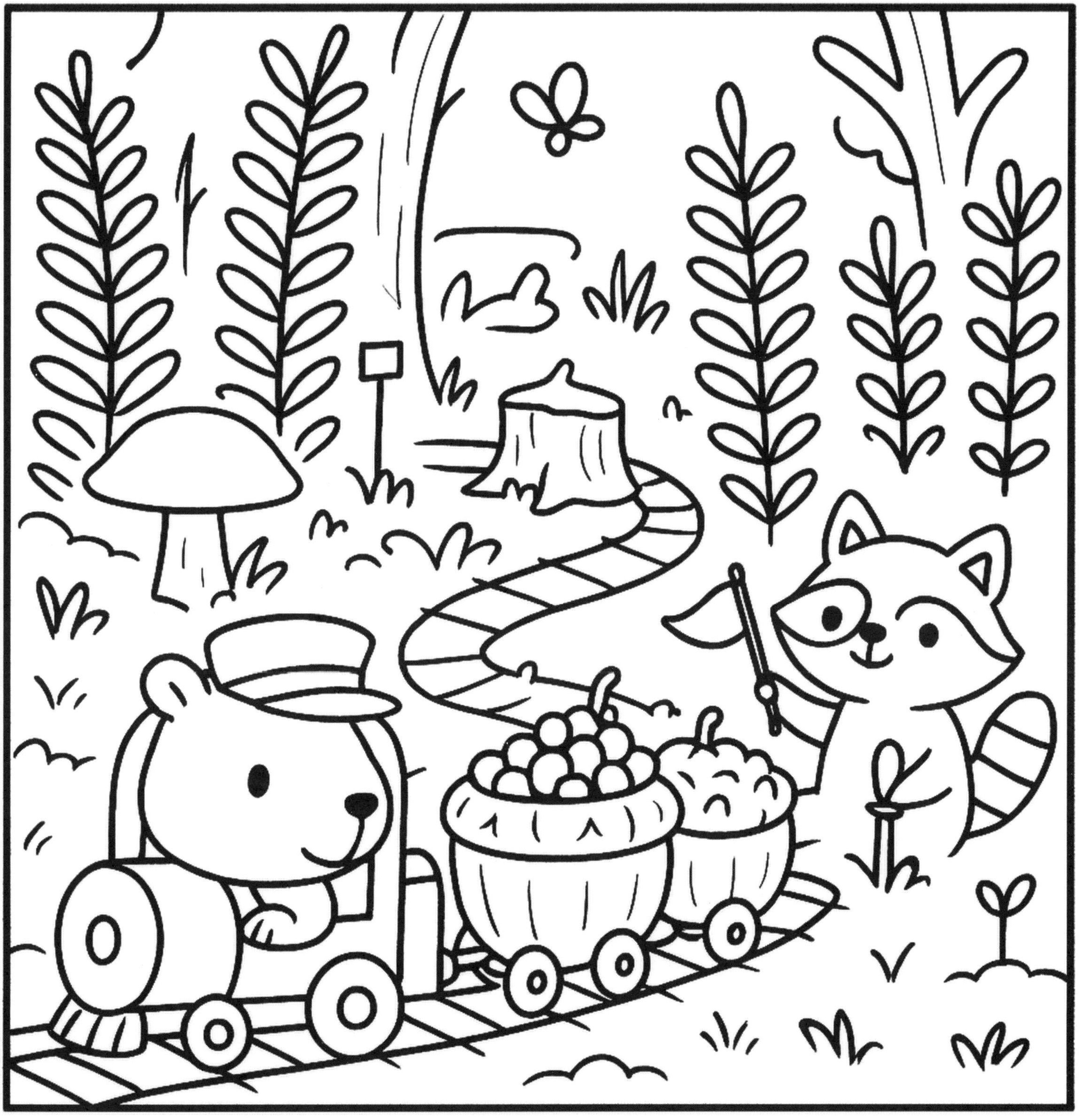

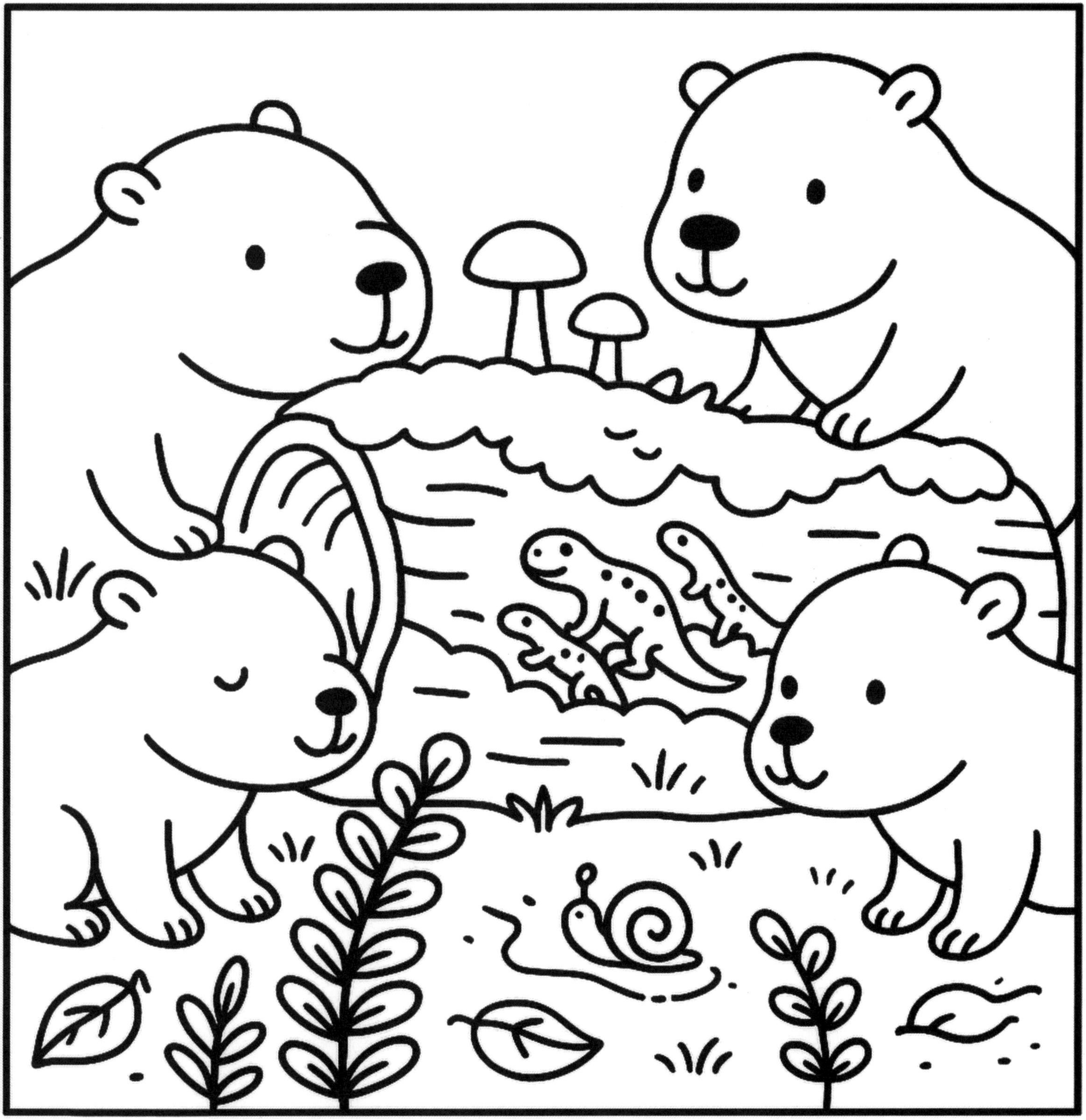

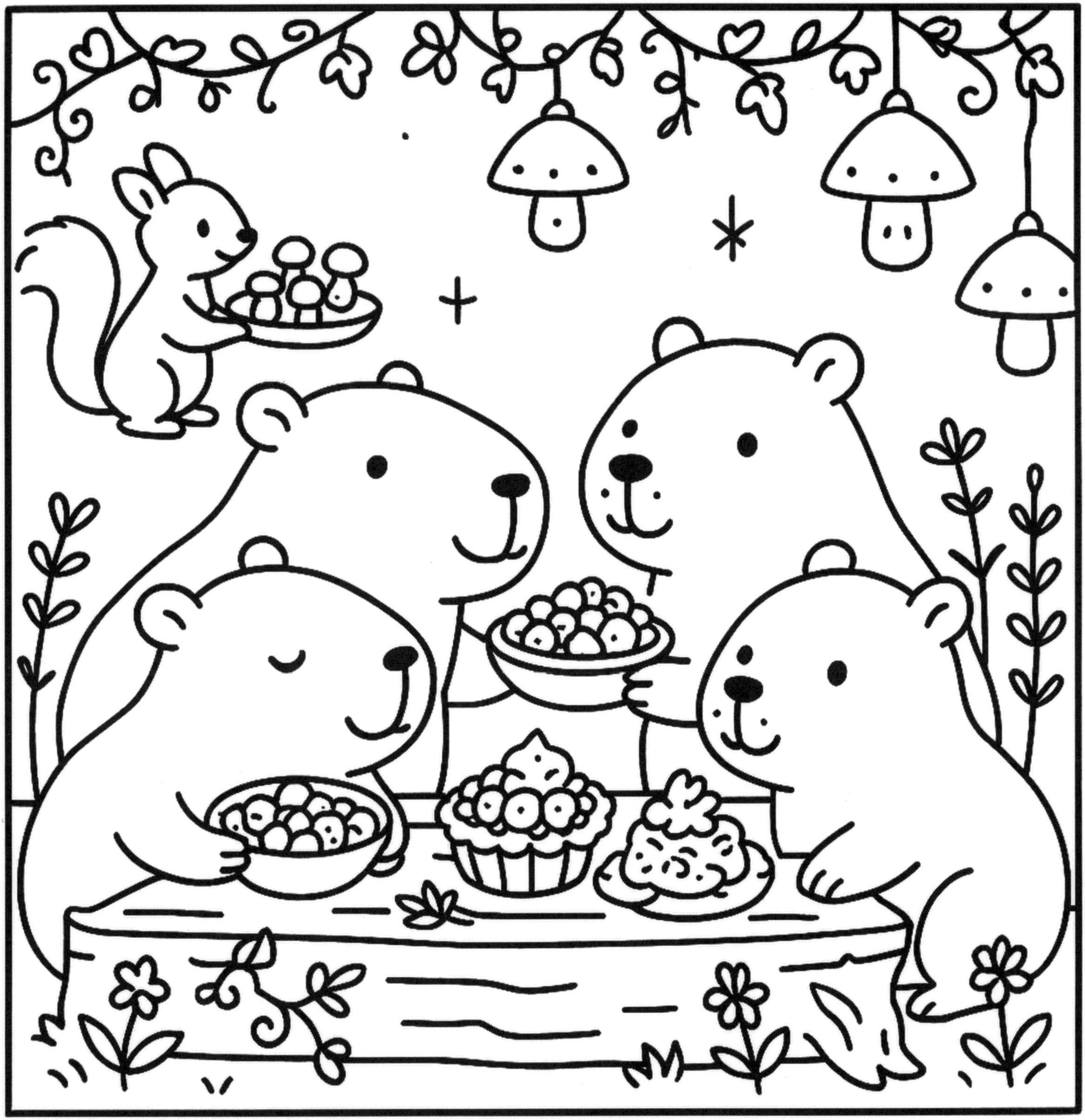

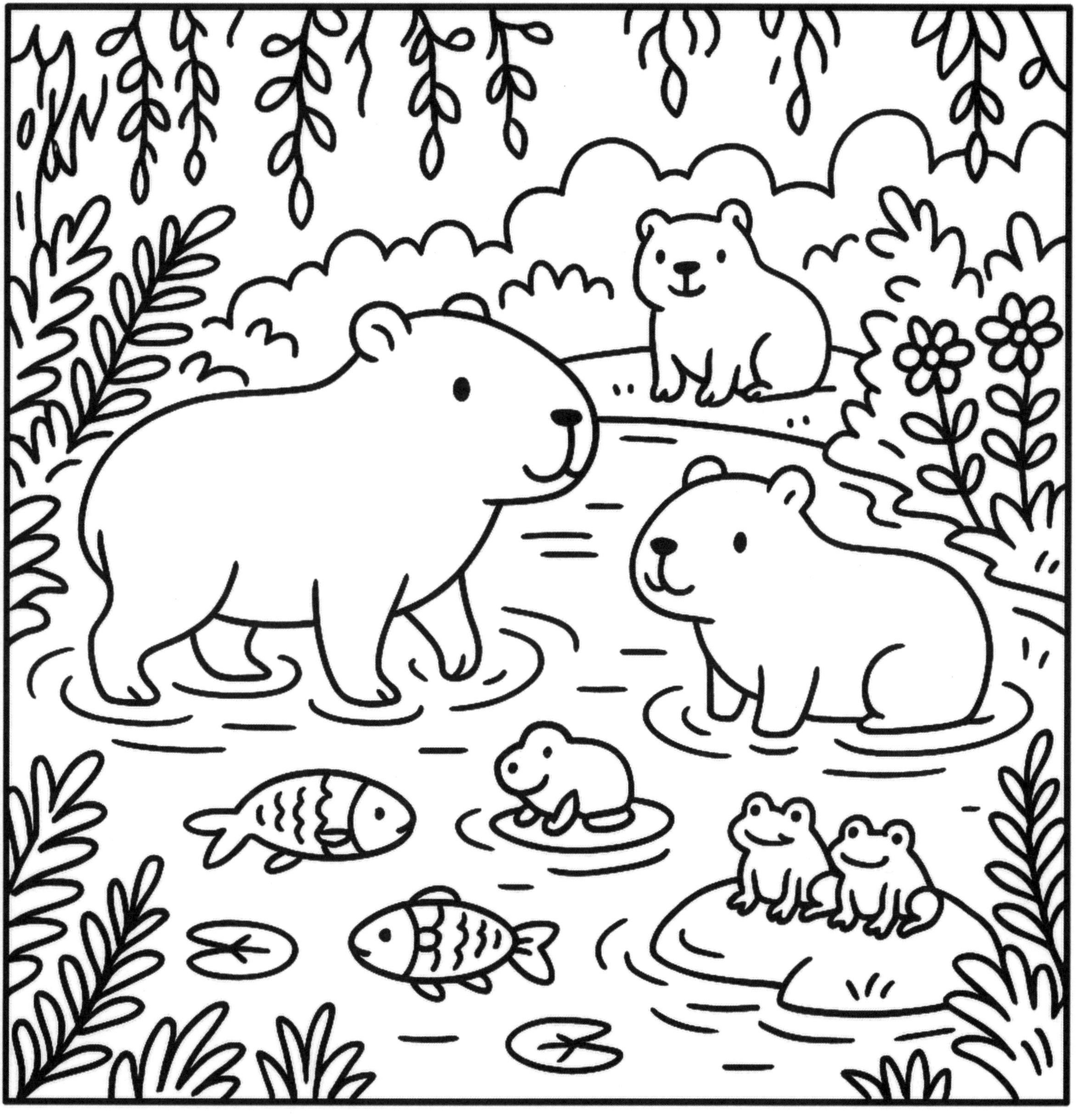

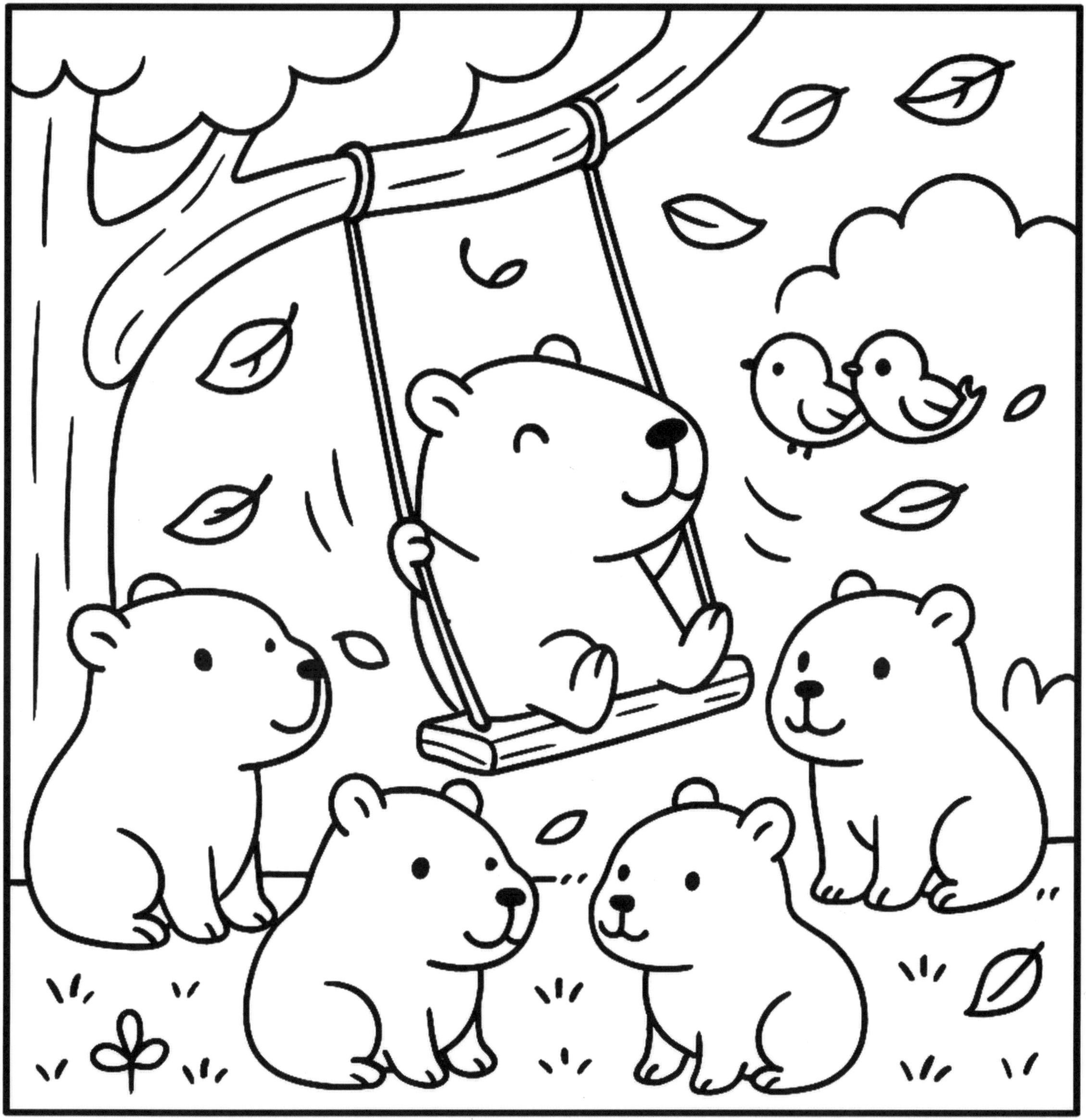

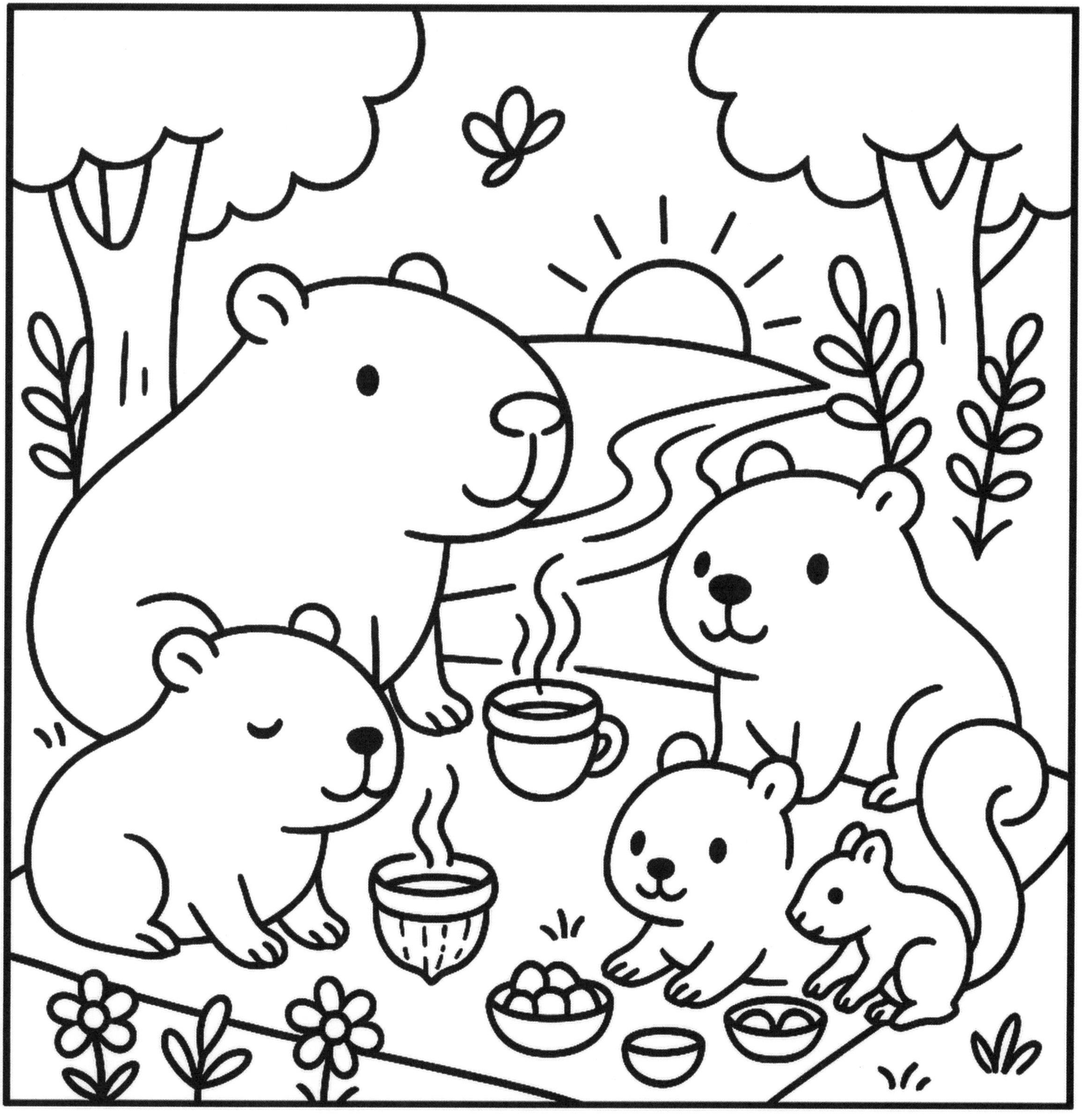

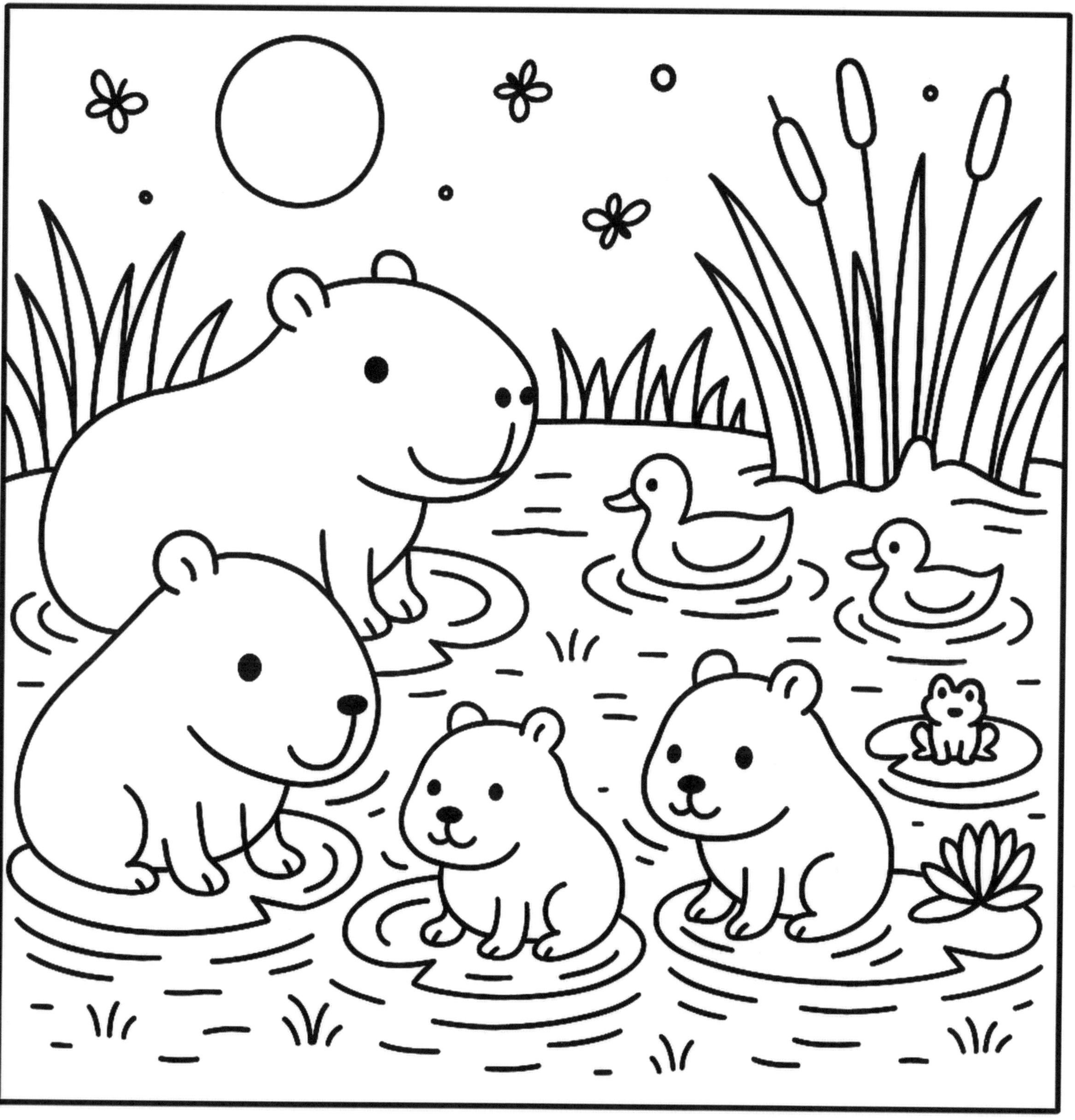

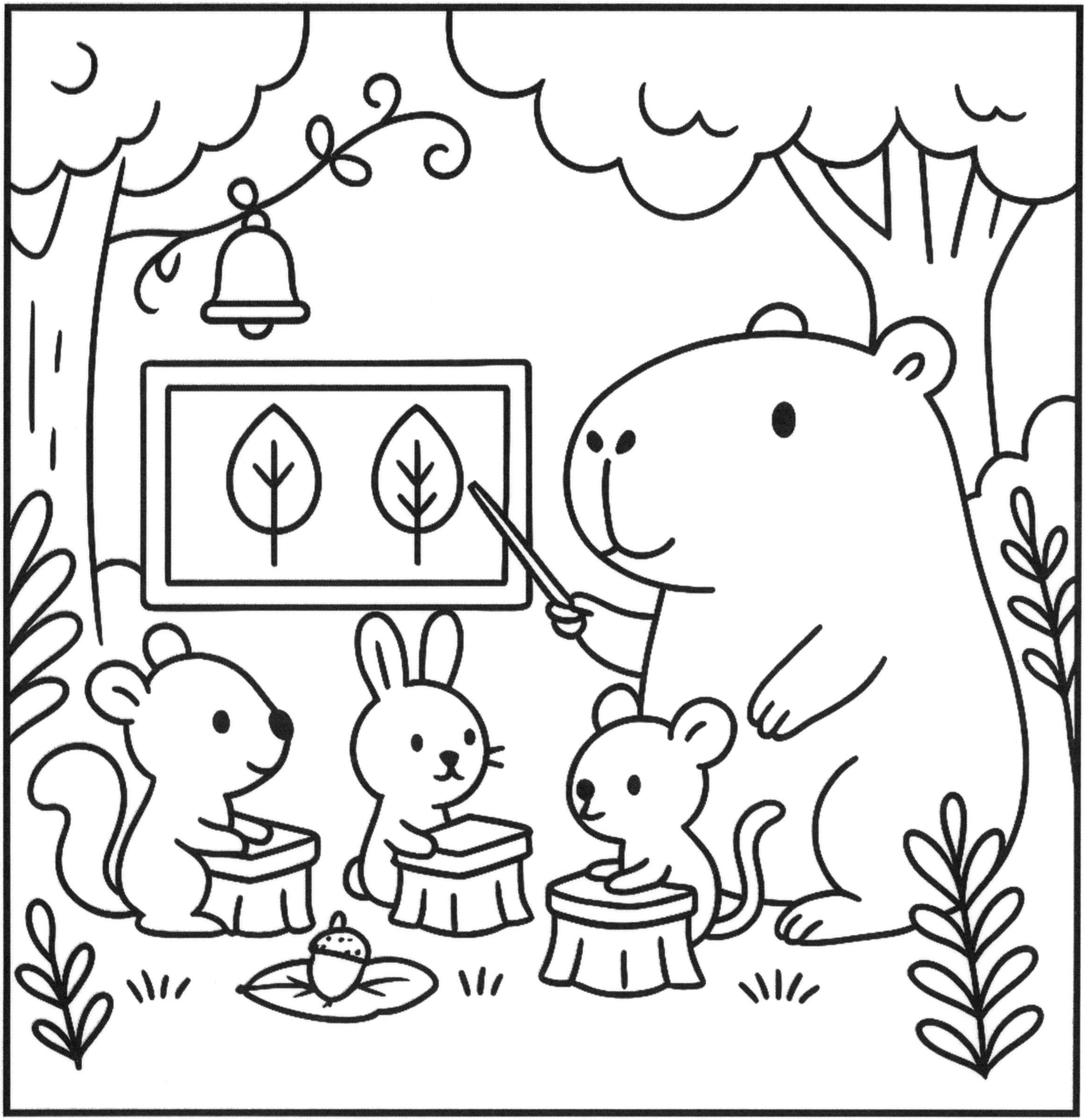

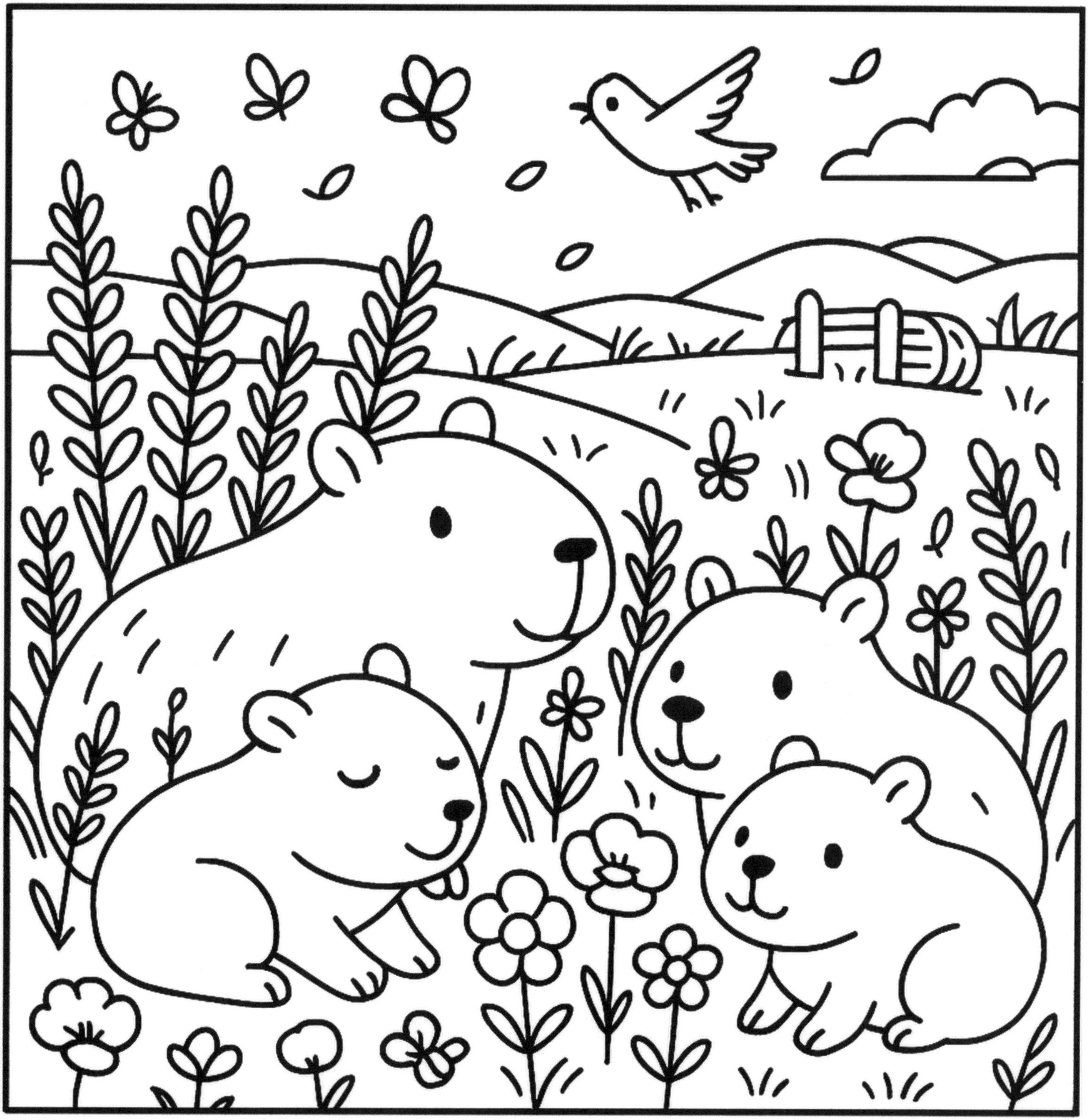

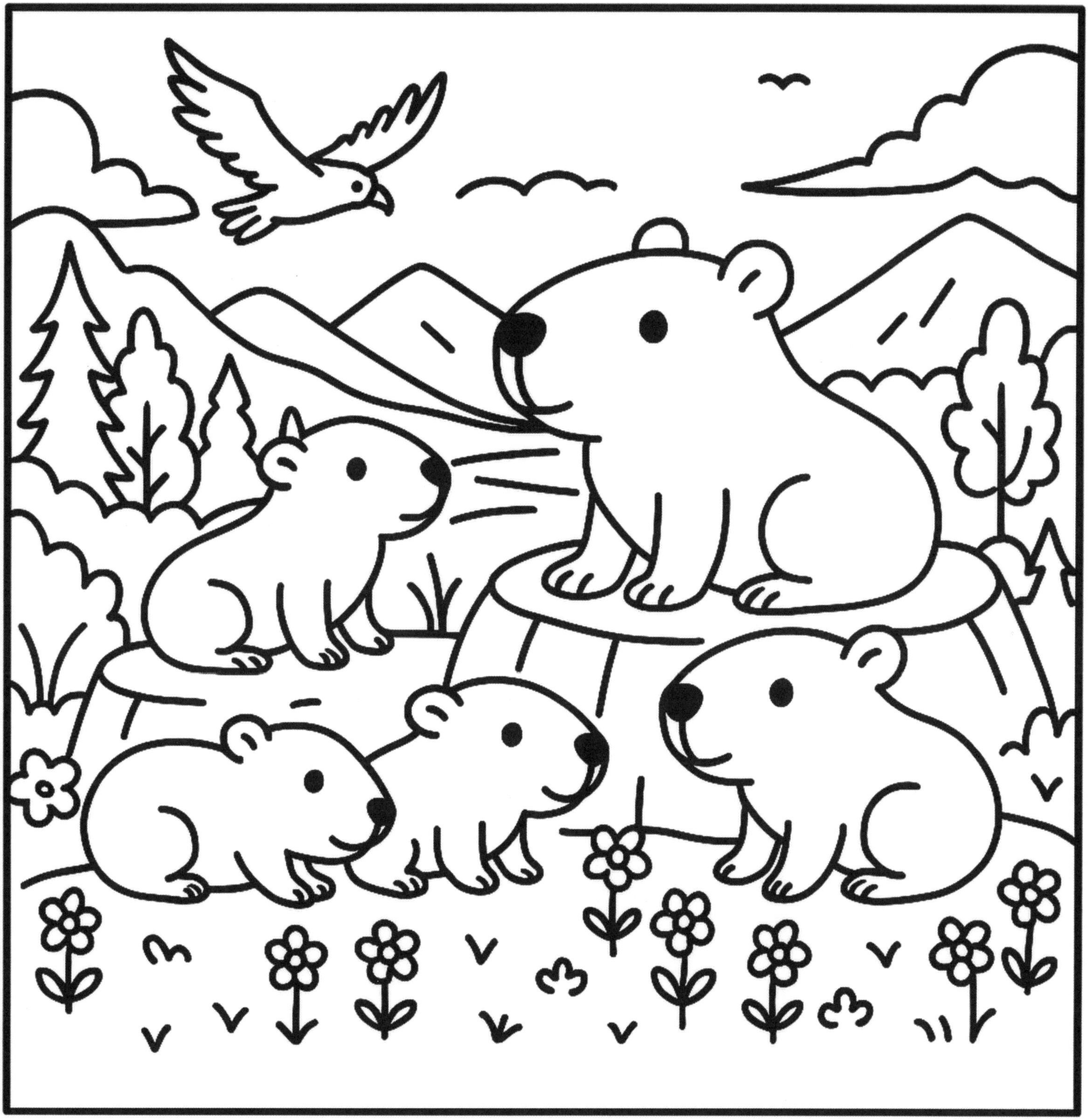

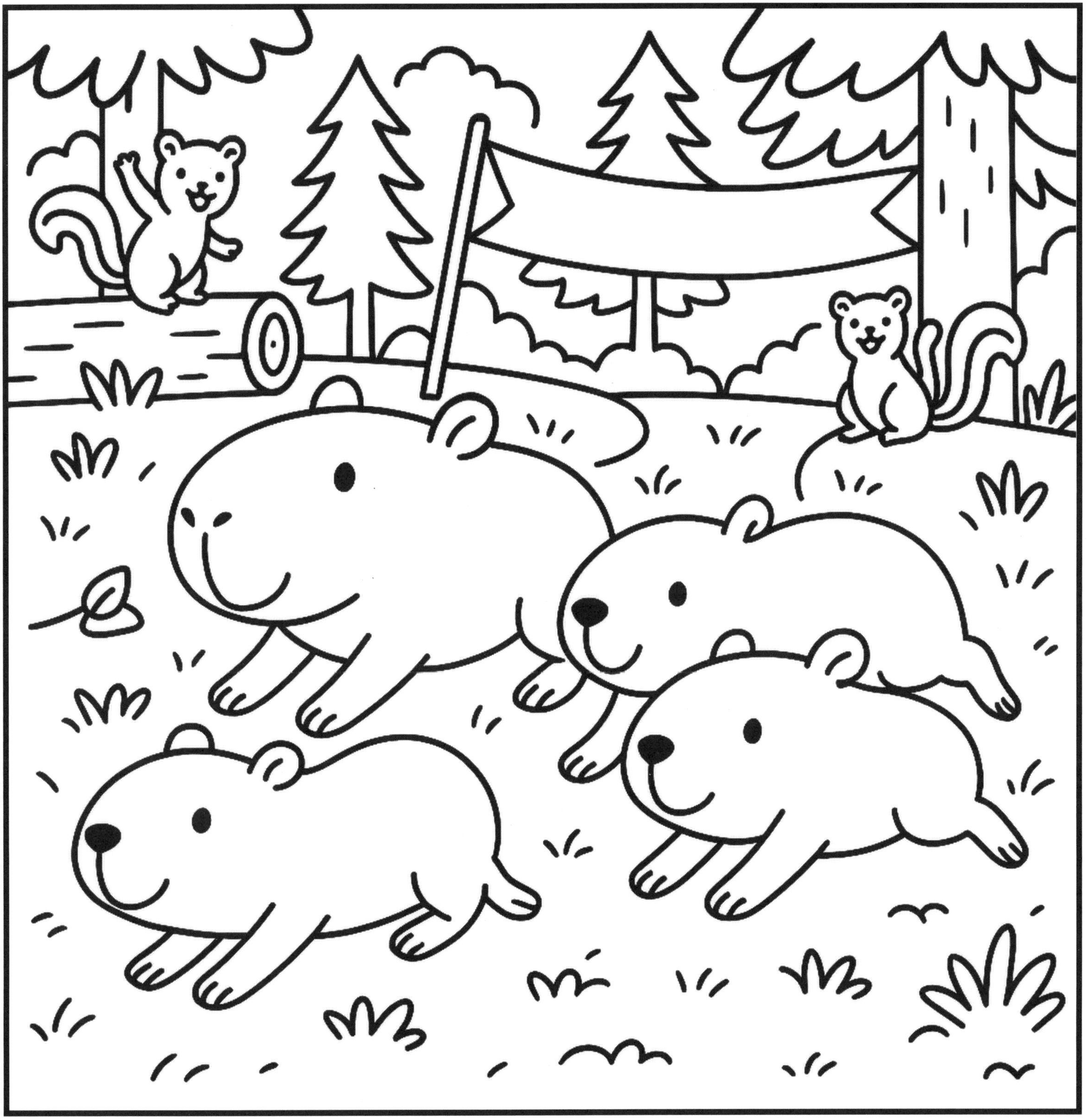

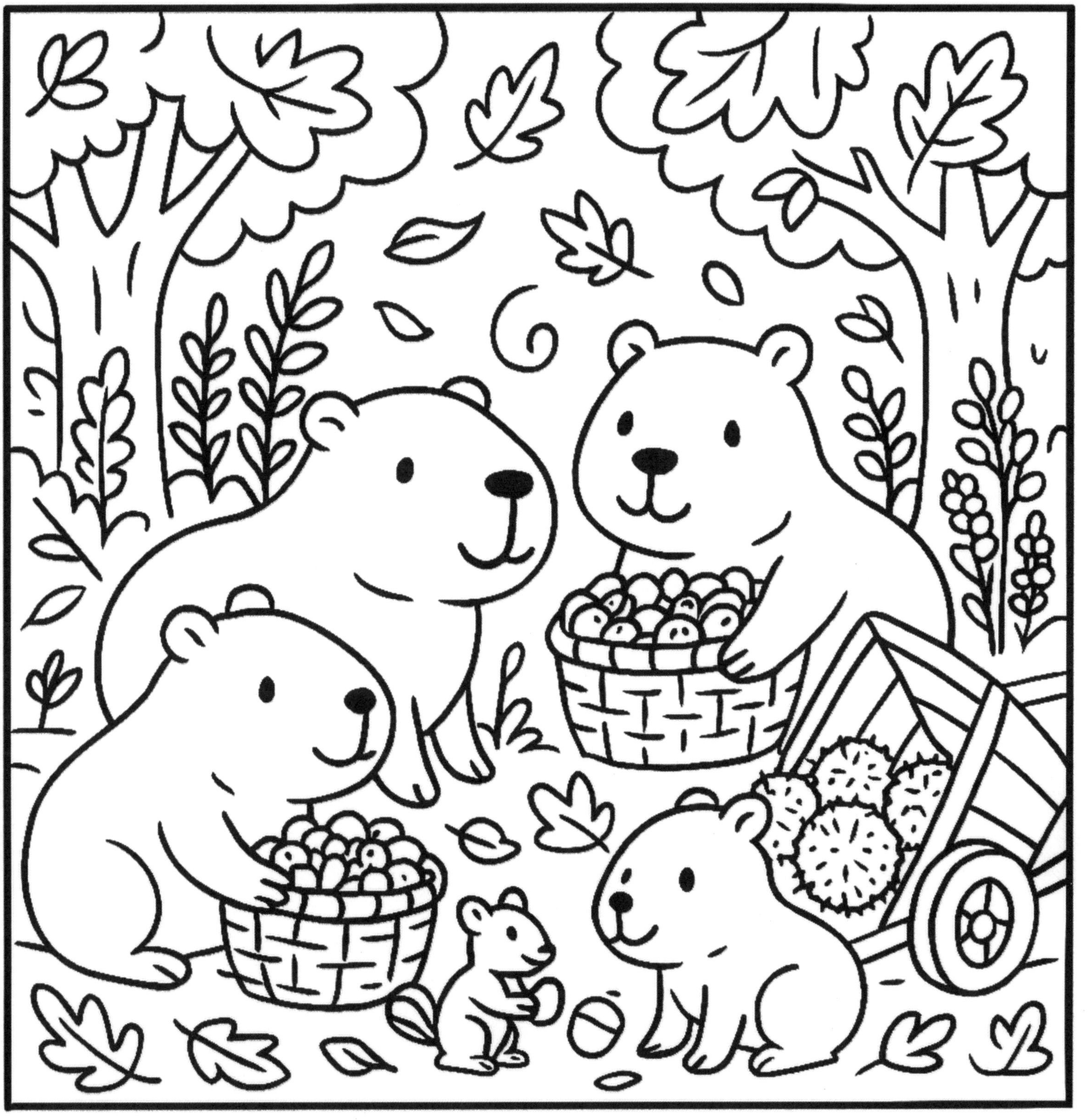

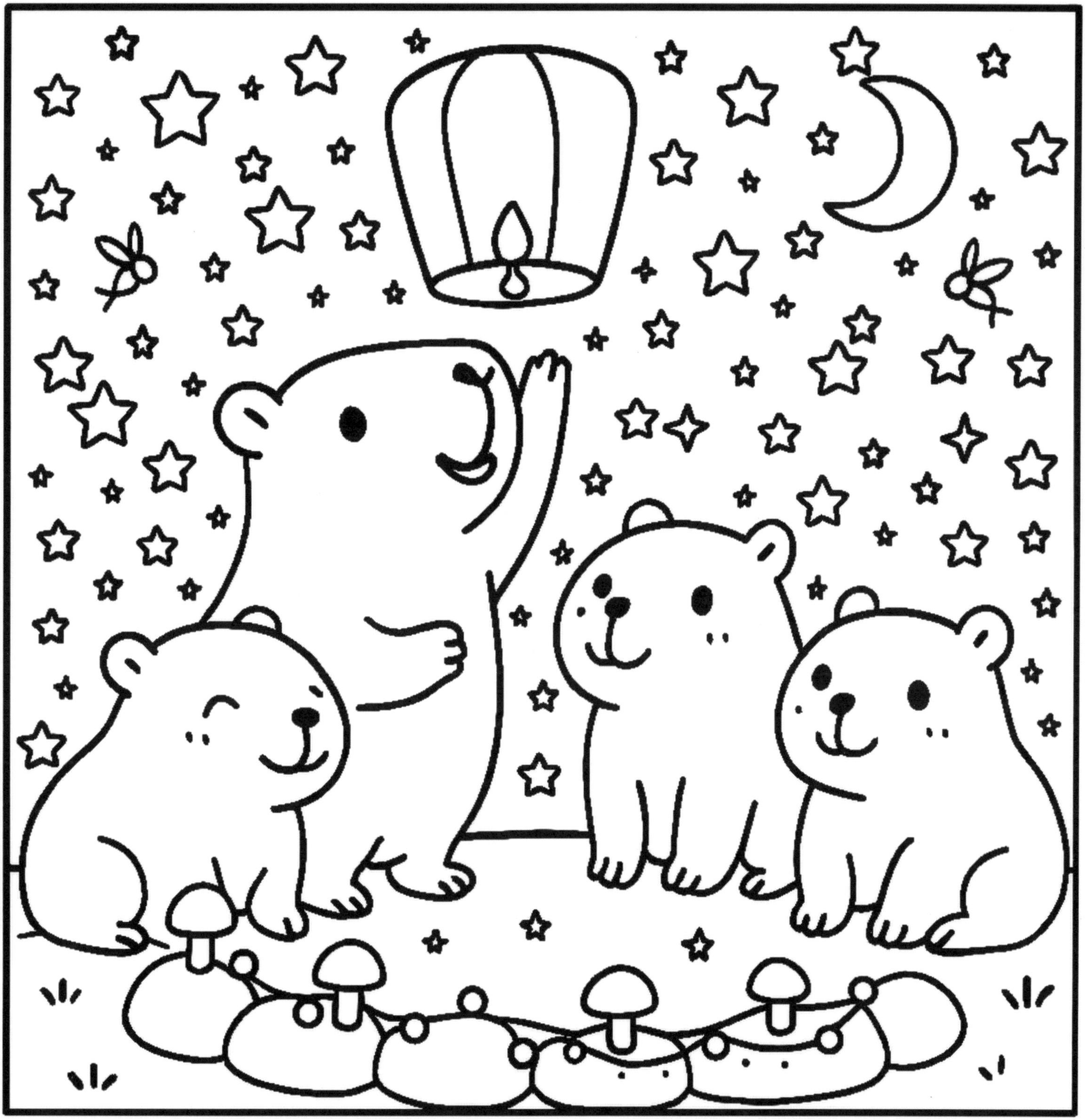